Progressive
GUITAR METHOD
Fingerpicking Guitar

by
Gary Turner

D1613928

CONTENTS

CONTENTS cont.

INTRODUCTION

The *Progressive Guitar Method* is a series of books designed to take the Guitar student from a beginner level through to a professional standard of playing. All books are carefully graded, lesson by lesson methods which assume no prior knowledge on your behalf. Within the series all styles and techniques of guitar playing are covered, including reading music, playing chords and rhythms, lead guitar and fingerpicking patterns.

Progressive Guitar Method: Fingerpicking Guitar assumes that you have a basic knowledge of guitar. You will need to know the notes on the first 3 frets of all 6 strings (the open position), basic timing, chords and key signatures.

All this information is contained in the book *Progressive Guitar Method: Book 1*. We recommend studying this book as it contains information that all guitarists should know.

Progressive Guitar Method: Fingerpicking Guitar will introduce you to right hand fingerpicking patterns that can be applied to any chord, chord progression or song. Playing chord shapes with these patterns will allow you to provide accompaniment for any song. After completing this book you will have a solid understanding of fingerpicking and may wish to study more advanced fingerpicking styles such as Ragtime, Classical and Flamenco. See *Progressive Classical Guitar Method, Progressive Fingerpicking Guitar Licks and Progressive Fingerpicking Guitar Solos*.

The best and fastest way to learn is to use these books in conjunction with:
1. Buying sheet music and song books of your favourite recording artists and learning to play their songs.
2. Practicing and playing with other musicians. You will be surprised how good a basic drums/bass/guitar combination can sound even when playing easy music.
3. Learning by listening to your favourite CDs.

APPROACH TO PRACTICE

From the beginning you should set yourself a goal. Many people learn guitar because of a desire to play like their favourite artist (e.g. Eric Clapton), or to play a certain style of music (e.g. Rock, Blues etc.). Motivations such as these will help you to persevere through the more difficult sections of work. As you develop it will be important to adjust and update your goals.

It is important to have a correct approach to practice. You will benefit more from several short practices (e.g. 15-30 minutes per day) than one or two long sessions per week. This is especially so in the early stages, because of the basic nature of the material being studied. In a practice session you should divide your time evenly between the study of new material and the revision of past work. It is a common mistake for semi-advanced students to practice only the pieces they can already play well. Although this is more enjoyable, it is not a very satisfactory method of practice. You should also try to correct mistakes and experiment with new ideas. It is the author's belief that an experienced teacher will be an invaluable aid to your progress.

Guitar Method
Book 1

A comprehensive, lesson by lesson introduction to the guitar, covering notes on all 6 strings, reading music, picking technique, basic music theory and incorporating well known traditional pop/rock, folk and blues songs.

Guitar Method
Book 2

A comprehensive, lesson by lesson method covering the most important keys and scales for guitar, with special emphasis on bass note picking, bass note runs, hammer-ons etc. Featuring chordal arrangements of well known Rock, Blues, Folk and Traditional songs.

Guitar Method
Book 1: Supplement

A collection of over 70 well known songs with chord symbols which can be used along or in conjunction with Progressive Guitar Method Book 1. Contains 8 more lessons on major scales, keys, triplets, 6/8 time, 16th notes, syncopation and swing rhythms.

Guitar Method
Theory Book 1

A comprehensive, introduction to music theory as it applies to the guitar. Covers reading traditional music, rhythm notation and tablature, along with learning the notes on the fretboard, how to construct chords and scales, transposition, musical terms and playing in all keys.

Guitar Method
Rhythm

Introduces all the important open chord shapes for major, minor, seventh, sixth, major seventh, minor seventh, suspended, diminished and augmented chords. Learn to play over 50 chord progressions, including 12 Bar Blues and Turnaround progressions.

Guitar Method
Lead

Covers scales and patterns over the entire fretboard so that you can improvise against major, minor, and Blues progressions in any key. Learn the licks and techniques used by all lead guitarists such as hammer-ons, slides, bending, vibrato, and more.

Guitar Method
Chords

Contains the most useful open, Bar and Jazz chord shapes of the most used chord types with chord progressions to practice and play along with. Includes sections on tuning, how to read sheet music, transposing, as well as an easy chord table, formula and symbol chart.

Guitar Method
Bar Chords

Introduces the most useful Bar, Rock and Jazz chord shapes used by all Rock/Pop/Country and Blues guitarist. Includes major, minor, seventh, sixth, major seventh, etc. Suggested rhythm patterns including percussive strums, dampening and others are also covered.

These titles are also available on video and DVDs.
For more information on the *Progressive* series see page 71 and contact;
Learn to Play Music
email: info@learntoplaymusic.com
or visit our website;
www.learntoplaymusic.com

Fingerpicking is most commonly played on **acoustic guitars**, however, all the styles and techniques outlined in this book can also be applied to the **electric guitar.**

ACOUSTIC GUITARS

CLASSICAL GUITAR
(Nylon Strings)

STEEL STRING ACOUSTIC

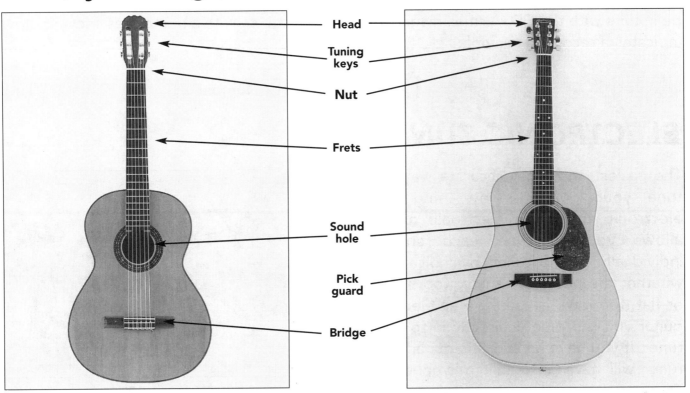

Head

Tuning keys

Nut

Frets

Sound hole

Pick guard

Bridge

The **classical** guitar has nylon strings and a wider neck than the other types of guitar. It is most commonly used for playing Classical, Flamenco and Fingerstyles. Generally it is much cheaper than other types of guitar and is recommended for beginning guitarists.

The **steel string acoustic** guitar has steel strings and is most commonly played by strumming or fingerpicking groups of notes called chords. This is the type of acoustic guitar you will hear in most modern styles of music e.g. Top 40 Rock and Pop music.

STRINGS

It is important to have the correct set of strings fitted to your guitar, especially if you are a beginner. Until you build enough strength in your hands to fret the chords cleanly, light gauge or low tension strings are recommended. A reputable music store which sells guitar strings should be able to assist with this. Do not put steel strings on a classical guitar or it will damage the neck of the guitar.

USING THE COMPACT DISC

It is recommended that you have a copy of the accompanying compact disc that includes all the examples in this book. The book shows you where to put your fingers and what technique to use and the recording lets you hear how each example should sound. Practice the examples slowly at first, gradually increasing tempo. Once you are confident you can play the example evenly without stopping the beat, try playing along with the recording. You will hear a drum beat at the beginning of each example, to lead you into the example and to help you keep time. To play along with the CD your guitar must be in tune with it (see below). If you have tuned using an electronic tuner your guitar will already be in tune with the CD. A small diagram of a compact disc with a number as shown below indicates a recorded example.

 **12.** ← CD Track Number

ELECTRONIC TUNER

The easiest and most accurate way to tune your guitar is by using an **electronic tuner**. An electronic tuner allows you to tune each string individually to the tuner, by indicating whether the notes are sharp (too high) or flat (too low). If you have an electric guitar you can plug it directly in to the tuner. If you have an acoustic guitar the tuner will have an inbuilt microphone. There are several types of electronic

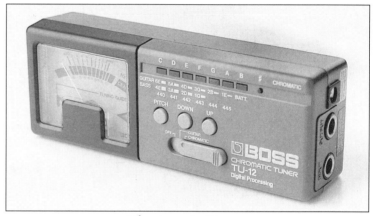
Electronic Tuner

guitar tuners but most are relatively inexpensive and simple to operate. Tuning using other methods is difficult for beginning guitarists and it takes many months to master, so we recommend you purchase an electronic tuner, particularly if you do not have a guitar teacher or a friend who can tune it for you. Also if your guitar is way out of tune you can always take it to your local music store so they can tune it for you. Once a guitar has been tuned correctly it should only need minor adjustments before each practice session. To learn to tune the guitar using other methods see *Progressive Guitar Method: Book 1*.

TUNING YOUR GUITAR TO THE CD

Before you commence each lesson or practice session you will need to tune your guitar. If your guitar is out of tune everything you play will sound incorrect even though you are holding the correct notes. On the accompanying CD the **first six tracks** correspond to the **six strings of the guitar**.

 **1 6th String**
E Note
(Thickest string)

 **2 5th String**
A Note

 **3 4th String**
D Note

4 3rd String
G Note

 **5 2nd String**
B Note

 **6 1st String**
E Note
(Thinnest string)

HOW TO READ MUSIC

There are two methods used to write guitar music. First is the **traditional music notation** (using music notes, ♩) and second is **Tablature**. Both are used in this book but you need only use one of these methods. Most guitarists find Tablature easier to read, however, it is very worthwhile to learn to read traditional music notation as well. Nearly all sheet music you buy in a store is written in traditional notation. To learn to read traditional music notation, see *Progressive Guitar Method 1*.

TABLATURE

Tablature is a method of indicating the position of notes on the fretboard. There are **six** "tab" lines each representing one of the six strings of the guitar. Study the following diagram.

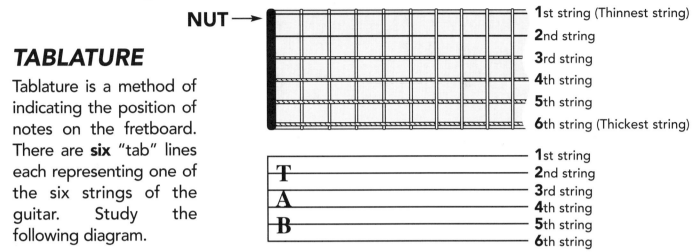

NUT →

1st string (Thinnest string)
2nd string
3rd string
4th string
5th string
6th string (Thickest string)

1st string
2nd string
3rd string
4th string
5th string
6th string

When a number is placed on one of the lines, it indicates the fret location of a note e.g.

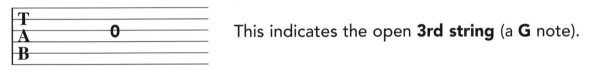

This indicates the open **3rd string** (a **G** note).

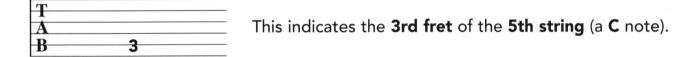

This indicates the **3rd fret** of the **5th string** (a **C** note).

CHORD DIAGRAMS

Chords are learnt with the help of a **chord diagram**. This will show you exactly where to place your left hand fingers in order to play a particular chord. A chord diagram is a grid of horizontal and vertical lines representing the strings and frets of the guitar as shown below.

LEFT HAND FINGERING

❶ Index Finger
❷ Middle Finger
❸ Ring Finger
❹ Little Finger

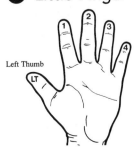

Left Thumb

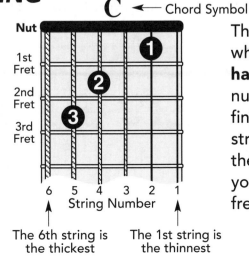

C ← Chord Symbol

Nut
1st Fret
2nd Fret
3rd Fret

6 5 4 3 2 1
String Number

The 6th string is the thickest

The 1st string is the thinnest

The **black** dots show you where to place your **left hand fingers**. The **white** number tells you which finger to place down on the string just behind the fret. If there is no dot on a string, you play it as an **open** (not fretted) string.

PRACTICE POSITION

Practice fingerpicking guitar styles by sitting with your right leg crossed or by using a foot stand as shown in the two photographs below. The guitar should be close to your body in an upright position with the neck of the guitar pointing slightly upwards.

LEFT HAND POSITION

The left hand fingers are numbered as such:

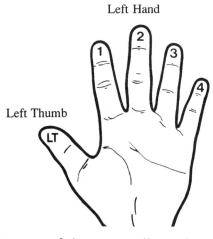

LEFT HAND PLACEMENT

Your fingers should be **ON THEIR TIPS** and placed just **BEHIND** the frets (not on top of them).

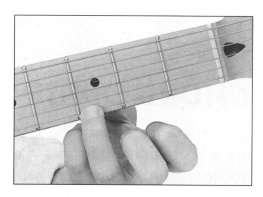

Photo A: CORRECT

Be careful not to allow the thumb to hang too far over the top of the neck (Photo B), or to let it run parallel along the back of the neck (Photo C).

Photo B: INCORRECT

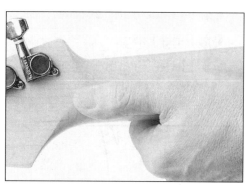

Photo C: INCORRECT

RIGHT ARM POSITION

The correct position for your right arm is shown in the photograph below. Notice that your forearm rests on the **upper edge** of the guitar, just below the elbow. Be careful not to have your elbow hanging over the face of the guitar, or your right hand too far along the fretboard.

CORRECT   **INCORRECT**

RIGHT HAND POSITION

Study the photographs below for the correct hand position.

1.   Rest the **forearm** on the upper edge of the guitar.

2.   The **right hand** is at 90 degrees to the strings.

3.   The **thumb** is parallel with the strings and clear of the other fingers.

4.   **Pick** the strings over the Sound hole for the best sound.

5.   **Do not** rest any part of your hand or fingers on the guitar body.

FRONT VIEW   **SIDE VIEW**

LESSON ONE

PICKING THE STRINGS

It is best to fingerpick the strings with your **fingernails** as this gives a better sound. You should let the fingernails of your right hand grow to a length that is comfortable for your playing e.g. 1/16" (1 millimetre) clear of the fingertip. The thumb nail should be longer. Fingernails should be shaped using a nail file (emery board) so that they have a rounded edge and flow smoothly off the string after it has been picked.

RIGHT HAND FINGER NAMES

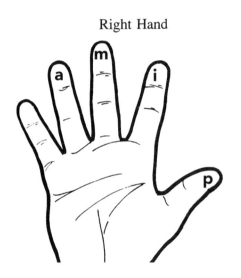

Right Hand

The right hand fingers are named using the following fingering symbols.

p = primary

i = index

m = middle

a = anular (ring finger)

The little finger is not used in fingerpicking.

PICKING WITH YOUR RIGHT HAND FINGERS

Start with your fingers not touching the strings, then pick the first string with your index finger (**i**) with an **upward** motion (do not pull the string outwards). Your finger should move from the first finger joint below the knuckle as shown in the diagram below. The sound is produced by the fingertip and the nail striking the string simultaneously. Move only your fingers, not your hand. The **i**, **m** and **a** fingers usually pick the **1st**, **2nd** and **3rd** strings.

PICKING WITH YOUR THUMB

The **p** finger (**thumb**) usually picks the **6th**, **5th** and **4th** strings. Pick with the lower side of your thumb as shown in the photograph below on the right. Pick with a **downward** motion and keep the thumb rigid, i.e. do not bend it like you do when picking with your fingers.

 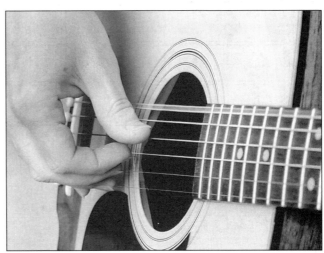

FINGERPICKING PATTERN 1

A **Fingerpicking pattern** is a set order of playing the strings. This same order of picking the strings is used with different chord shapes. The pattern is based upon the symbols given for each right hand finger.

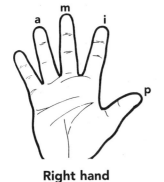

Right hand

The first fingerpicking pattern is:

Fingerpicking Pattern 1

Right hand finger →

p	i	m	i
Count → 1	+	2	+
String number → 5	2	1	2

Any pattern you learn can be applied to any chord you know. In the example below, **Fingerpicking Pattern 1** is played using a **C** major chord. This pattern occurs twice in 1 bar of $\frac{4}{4}$ time using eighth notes.

Fingerpicking Pattern 1

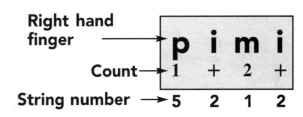

🎵 7

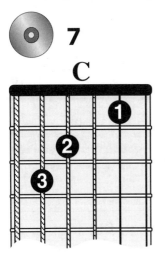

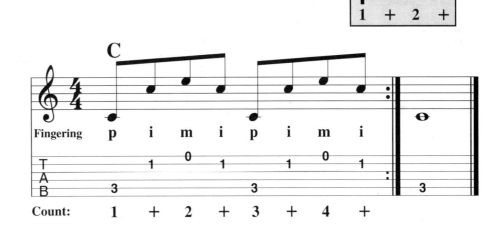

Apply fingerpicking pattern 1 to the chord progression below and use the following **C major**, **D seventh** and **G seventh** chord shapes.

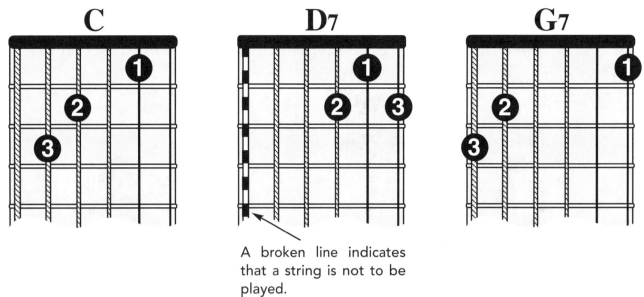

A broken line indicates that a string is not to be played.

THE PIVOT

When changing between the **C** and **D7** chords the first finger does not move. The note played by the first finger (a C note) is common to both chords. The second and third fingers move to their new position and the first finger acts as a **pivot**. The use of pivot fingers will make chord changes easier.

8

Fingerpicking Pattern 1

p	i	m	i
1	+	2	+

Always hold the complete chord shape even though you do not play every string.

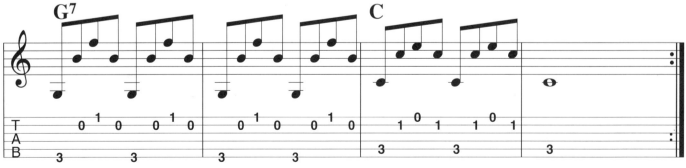

♯ This is a sharp sign. It indicates that a note on the stave is played one fret higher. If you are not familiar with this symbol see **Progressive Guitar Method 1.**

ALTERNATING BASS NOTES

The **root note** of a chord is the note after which the chord is named e.g:
• the root note of a **C** chord is **C**,
• the root note of a **G7** chord is **G**
• the root note of a **D7** chord is **D**.
In the previous example the thumb (**p**) played the root note of each chord as the bass note. To make picking patterns sound more interesting the bass note can alternate between the root note and another note in the chord.

The following example uses the same chord sequence as on the previous page but each chord lasts for one bar and is played using **alternating bass** notes. The fingerpicking pattern does not change and the thumb (**p**) plays the bass notes. As with any song or chord progression always hold the complete chord shape even though you might not pick every string.

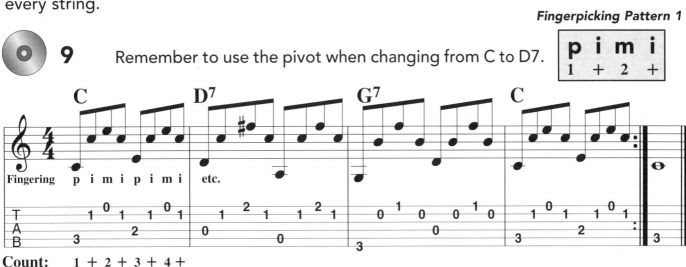

FINGERPICKING ACCOMPANIMENT

Chords are played to accompany a melody. The melody is sung or played by another musical instrument (eg, guitar, piano, etc). The chords can be strummed using a pick (playing all six strings together), or played fingerpicking style (playing one string at a time). Written below is the melody of a song called Aura Lee. You can play the chords by applying fingerpicking pattern 1 to them. The melody can be sung or played by another instrument. On the CD the melody has been played by another guitar so you can play along with it (accompany it).

10 Aura Lee

This example contains only the first four bars of the melody of this song. For a full version of **Aura Lee**, see lesson 5.

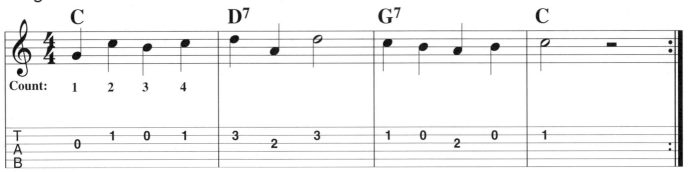

LESSON TWO

FINGERPICKING PATTERN 2

Fingerpicking Pattern **2** **Count**

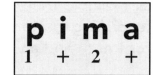

 11 Apply this new pattern to a **C** chord and alternate the bass. This pattern occurs twice in one bar of $\frac{4}{4}$ time using eighth notes.

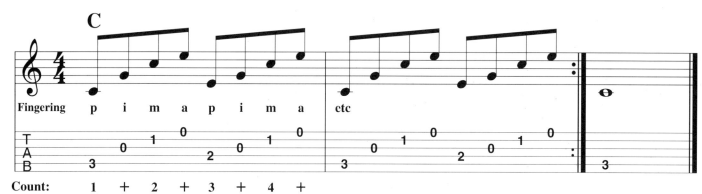

 ## 12 **Ode to joy**

This song is the melody of **Beethoven's 9th Symphony**. Use an alternating bass when playing the fingerpicking accompaniment. You can select any bass note on the **6th**, **5th** or **4th** string depending upon which one sounds the best. Generally you should start on the root note. Always hold the complete chord shape.

Fingerpicking Pattern 2

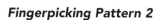
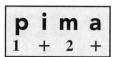

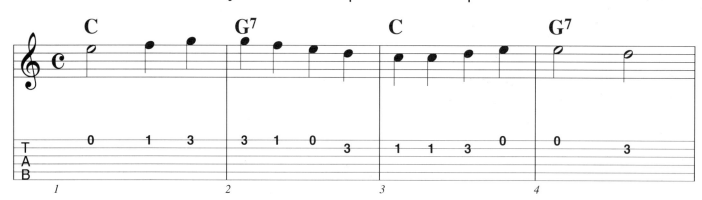

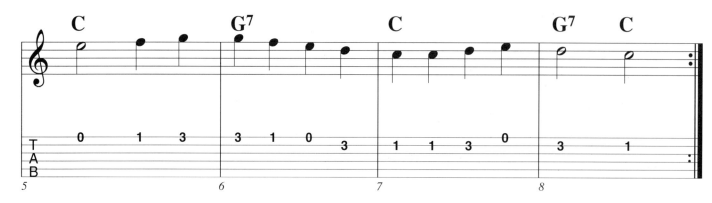

The chord progression written below is a **Turnaround** in the key of C major and uses the following **A minor** and **D minor** chord shapes. For more information on Turnarounds, see *Progressive Guitar Method: Book 1.*

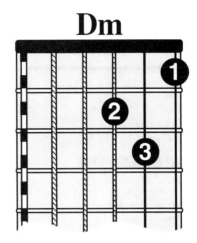

 13

When changing from **C** to **Am**, use your first and second fingers as pivots. You will only need to move your third finger when making this chord change. When changing from **Dm** to **G7**, use your first finger as a pivot.

Fingerpicking Pattern 2

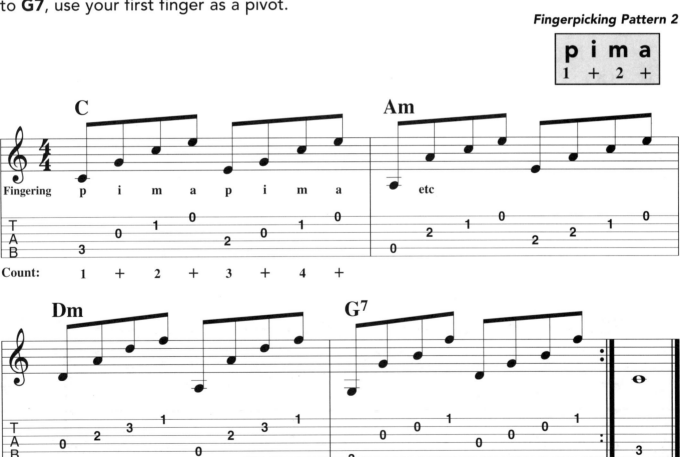

The chord progressions in examples 14 and 15 contain an **E minor** chord. This chord shape is usually played with the second and third fingers as shown below.

However, in example 14 the chord change between the **C** and **Em** chords will be made easier if you use the following alternative fingering. This will allow the second finger to act as a pivot and the third finger to move down to the second fret. Always look for alternate fingering and pivot fingers to make chord changes easier.

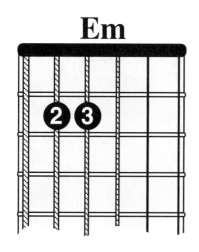

Fingerpicking Pattern 2

14

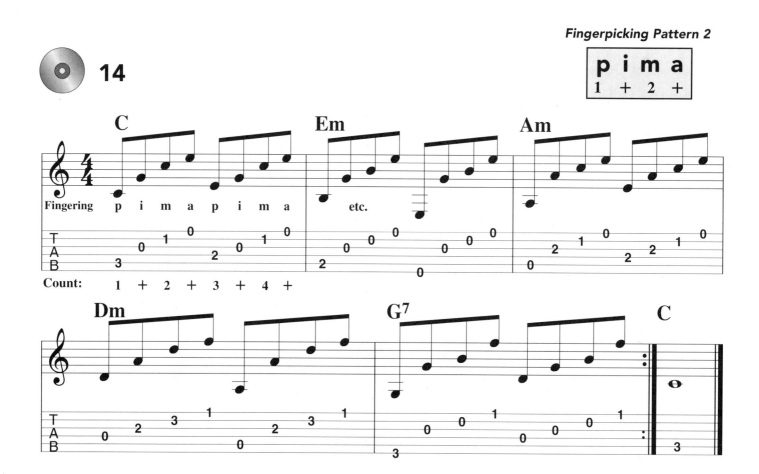

The following chord progression uses the **G major** chord shape as shown on the chord diagram below.

Written below is another fingering for the **E minor** chord. This alternative fingering will make the change between **G** to **Em** and **Em** to **C** easier by using the first finger as a pivot.

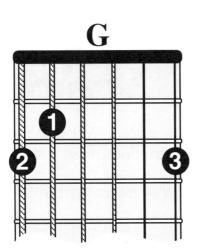

THE SLIDE FINGER

Another technique that can be used to make some chord changes easier is called the **slide finger**. Eg: when changing from **D7** to **G** in the example below, do not lift your third finger off the string, but slide it up to the third fret. Only touch the string very lightly as you do this. When changing from **G** to **D7**, slide your third finger down to the second fret.

In the following example, use pivot fingers between all chord changes and the slide finger when changing from **D7** back to **G**.

 15

The following progression is a Turnaround in the **key of G major**, so play all F notes as **F♯** as indicated by the key signature.

Fingerpicking Pattern 2

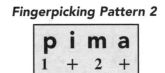

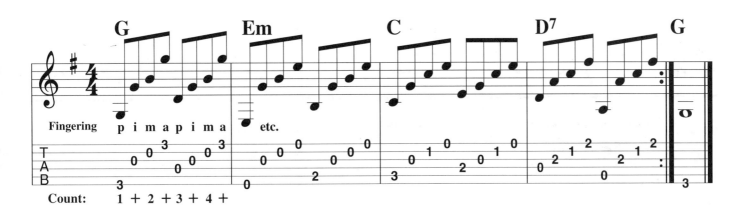

LESSON THREE

FINGERPICKING PATTERNS IN ¾ TIME

Fingerpicking Pattern 3

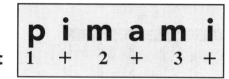

Count

 16

Here is this new pattern applied to the **C** chord with an alternating bass.

This pattern occurs once in one bar of ¾ time, so you can only alternate the bass note if the chord is played for more than one bar.

 17

The following chord progression uses fingerpicking pattern 3. The thumb (**p**) plays the root note of each chord. Make use of pivot fingers when changing from **C** to **Am** and **G7** to **Dm**.

Fingerpicking Pattern 3

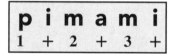

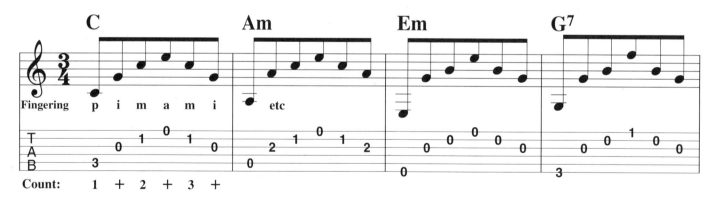

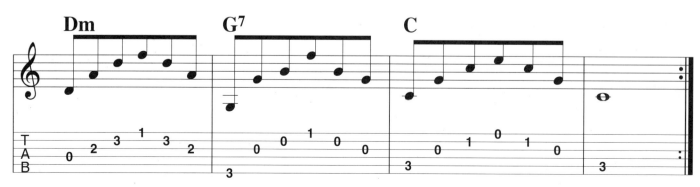

The following three songs are in ¾ time and use fingerpicking pattern 3.

18 Scarborough Fair

Use fingerpicking pattern 3 to accompany the melody of **Scarborough Fair**. This song is a folk music standard. When a chord is held for more than one bar, eg: **Am** in bars 1 and 2, alternate the bass to make the fingerpicking accompaniment more interesting. You may find the chord changes to and from **G** are easier if the **G** chord is played with the second, third and fourth fingers as an alternative fingering. The abbreviation *rit.* above bar 18 indicates to gradually slow down.

Fingerpicking Pattern 3

p	i	m	a	m	i
1	+	2	+	3	+

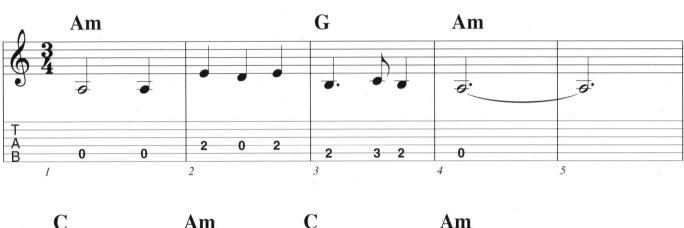

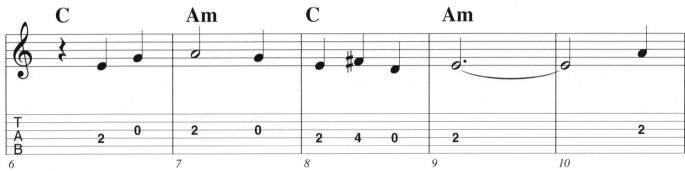

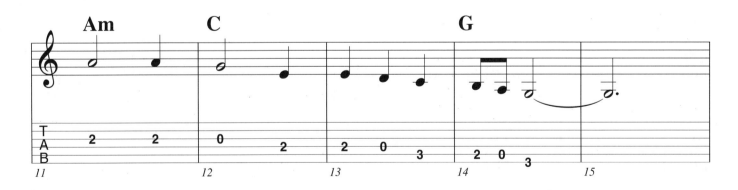

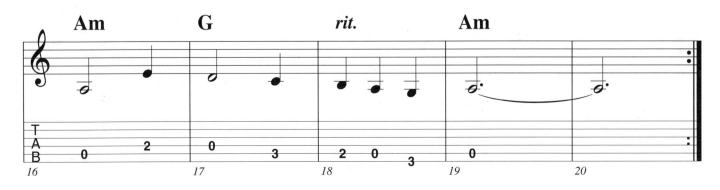

The song **Silent Night** uses the **F major** chord shape as shown in the chord diagram.

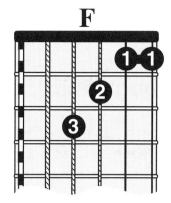

 19 Silent Night

Silent Night is one of the most popular christmas songs. Once again, use alternating bass notes when a chord is held for more than one bar. Play the bass notes that sound the best to you. Remember, as long as you are holding the chord shape the bass note will sound correct.

Fingerpicking Pattern 3

p	i	m	a	m	i
1	+	2	+	3	+

20 Morning Has Broken

When playing the accompaniment to this song, do not start picking until bar 2. Use a combination of root notes (for chords that are played for one bar) and alternate bass notes (for the chords that are held for more than one bar).

Fingerpicking Pattern 3

LESSON FOUR

PLAYING NOTES TOGETHER

When the right hand fingering symbols are placed on top of each other it indicates that they are played **together**. Eg: $\overset{a}{\underset{i}{m}}$ indicates that the **i**, **m** and **a** fingers play all three notes together.

The following fingerpicking pattern makes use of this technique.

Fingerpicking Pattern **4a** Count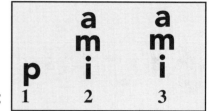

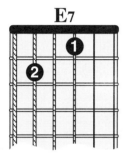

This pattern occurs once in one bar of ¾ time using quarter notes. The following example and the song **Greensleeves** use fingerpicking pattern 4a. They also use the **E seventh** chord as shown.

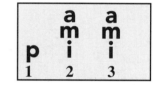
Fingerpicking Pattern 4a

 21

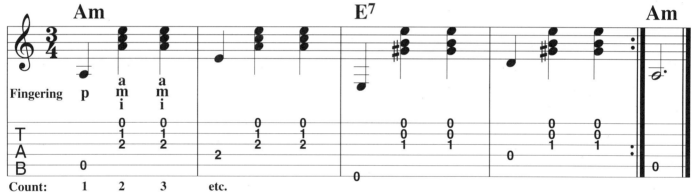

 22 Greensleeves

Greensleeves is an old English folk song and is in the key of A minor. For chords that are played for only one bar, use the root note as the bass note. For the chords held for more than one bar you can use the root note or alternate bass notes. Pick the bass notes that sound best to you.

Fingerpicking Pattern 4a

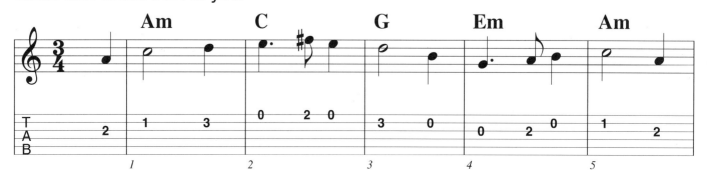

Fingerpicking Pattern 4b

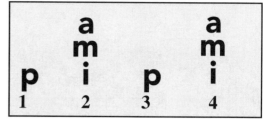

Count

p	a m i	p	a m i
1	2	3	4

The above pattern is in $\frac{4}{4}$ time and uses the same $\overset{a}{\underset{i}{m}}$ grouping as the previous pattern. This pattern occurs once in one bar of $\frac{4}{4}$ time using quarter notes.

 ## 23 Waltzing Matilda

Waltzing Matilda is the most well known song from Australia and is in the **key of G major**. Use fingerpicking pattern 4b to accompany this song. Use a combination of root notes and alternate picking in the bass.

24 Sakura

This is a well known folk song from Japan and is in the **key of A minor**. Use a combination of root notes and alternate picking in the bass.

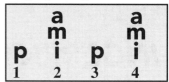

Fingerpicking Pattern 4a

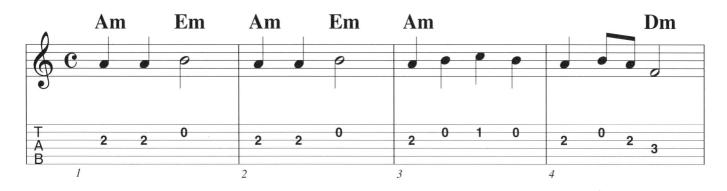

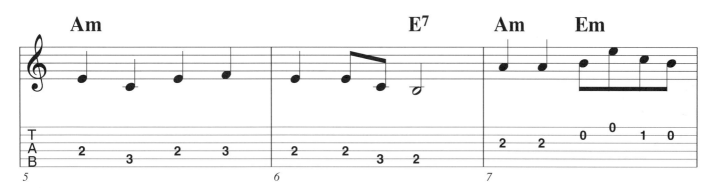

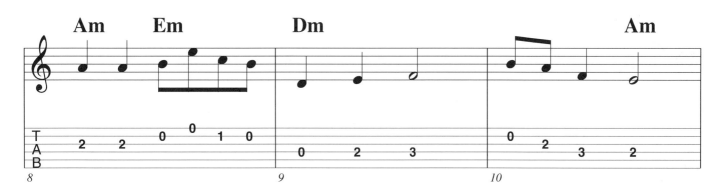

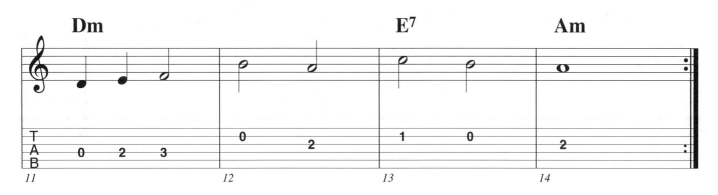

LESSON FIVE

FINGERPICKING PATTERN 5

Fingerpicking Pattern **5** Count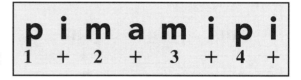

This pattern lasts for one full bar in 4/4 time and has two alternating bass notes played by the thumb (**p**) on the 1 and 4 count. Example 25 features 2 bars of pattern 5 applied to the **C** and **Am** chords.

 25

The following chord progression is a Turnaround in the **key of C Major** and uses fingerpicking pattern 5. Practice this new pattern holding a **C** chord, then play the entire progression.

Fingerpicking Pattern 5

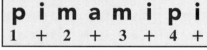

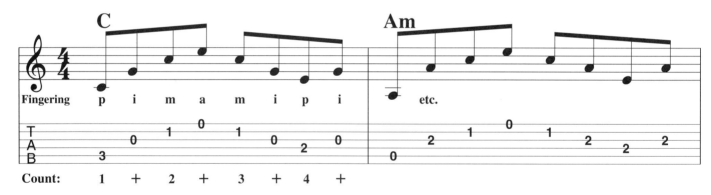

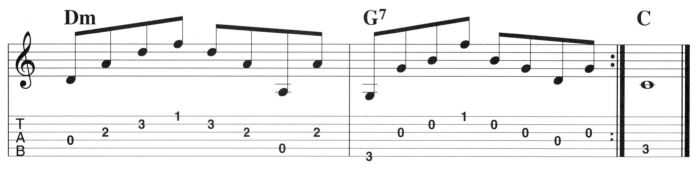

26 Sloop John B

This well known folk song uses fingerpicking pattern **5** and is in the key of **G major**.

27 Minuet

This song is in the key of G major and uses the **B minor** chord shown in the accompanying diagram.

This song is based upon a melody by famous classical composer **Bach.** Use fingerpicking pattern 5 when there is one chord per bar. Use fingerpicking pattern 2 when there are two chords per bar.

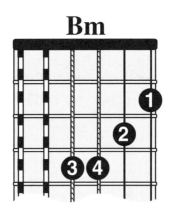

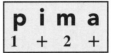

The song **Aura Lee** uses the following **A seventh** and **B seventh** chord shapes as shown in the chord diagrams below.

A7
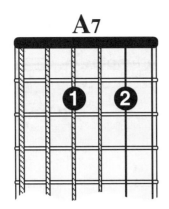

B7
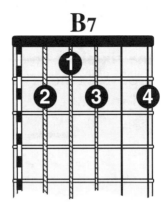

 ## 28 Aura Lee

On page 13 the first four bars of the song **Aura Lee** were given. Here is the complete version of this song in the **key of G major**. Use fingerpicking pattern 5 for all bars except bar 9. Use fingerpicking pattern 2 for bar 9. When changing between **B7** and **Em**, use your second finger as a pivot.

Fingerpicking Pattern 2
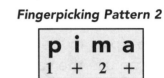

Fingerpicking Pattern 5
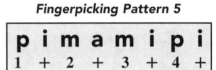

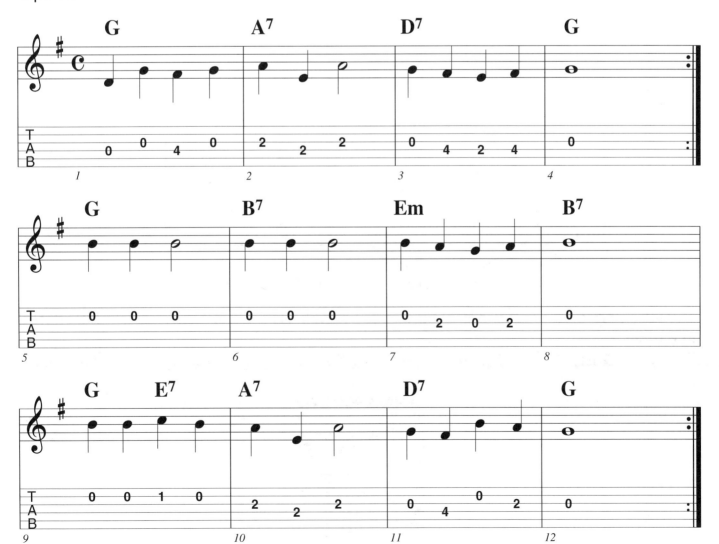

LESSON SIX

FINGERPICKING PATTERNS IN $\frac{6}{8}$ TIME

6
8 This is the **six eight** time signature. There are six eighth notes in one bar of $\frac{6}{8}$ time. The six eighth notes are divided into two groups of three.

Count: 1 2 3 4 5 6   or   1 2 3 4 5 6

When playing $\frac{6}{8}$ time there are two beats in each bar with each beat being a dotted quarter note. (This is different to $\frac{4}{4}$ time and $\frac{3}{4}$ time where each beat is a quarter note.) **Accent** (play louder) the 1 and 4 count to help establish the two beats per bar. Songs in $\frac{6}{8}$ time can use the same picking patterns as songs in $\frac{3}{4}$ time.

Fingerpicking Pattern 4a in $\frac{3}{4}$ time

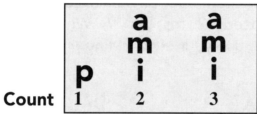

This pattern was introduced in an earlier lesson. It occurs once in one bar of $\frac{3}{4}$ time. In $\frac{6}{8}$ time the pattern occurs twice, as shown below.

Fingerpicking Pattern 4a in $\frac{6}{8}$ time

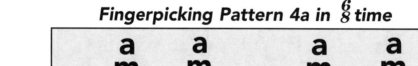

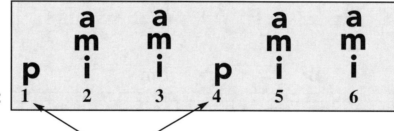

Accent (play louder) the **1** and **4** count.

The following three songs are in $\frac{6}{8}$ time and use fingerpicking patterns originally introduced in $\frac{3}{4}$ time.

The songs **Daisy Bell** and **House of the Rising Sun** use the **D major** chord shape as shown in the following chord diagram.

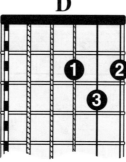

D

29 Daisy Bell (A Bicycle Built for Two)

This song is in the key of **G major** and is in ⅜ time. Use fingerpicking pattern **4a** in ⅜ time to accompany the melody. Use an alternating bass.

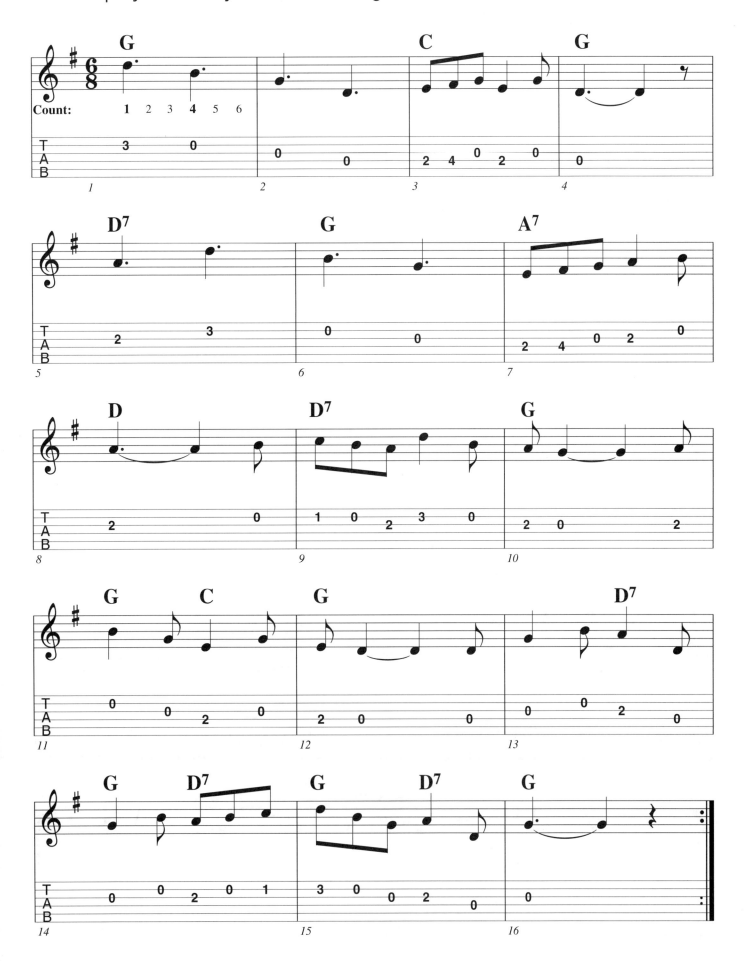

Fingerpicking pattern 3 introduced in Lesson 3 can also be played in $\frac{6}{8}$ time. It occurs once in one bar of $\frac{3}{4}$ time and once in one bar of $\frac{6}{8}$ time.

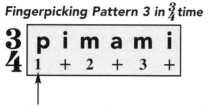

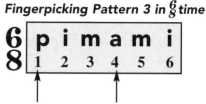

In $\frac{3}{4}$ time the accent is on the number 1.

In $\frac{6}{8}$ time the accent is on the numbers 1 and 4.

The next two songs are in $\frac{6}{8}$ time and use the above fingerpicking pattern.

 ## 30 House of the Rising Sun

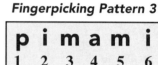

This song is in $\frac{6}{8}$ time and is in the **key of A minor**.

31 When Johnny Comes Marching Home

This song dates back to the American civil war. In bars 13 and 14 you can use the pattern shown below as an alternative to help emphasize the chord changes.

LESSON SEVEN

CLAWHAMMER

One of the most useful and popular fingerpicking patterns is called **Clawhammer**. The basic clawhammer pattern is:

Fingerpicking Pattern **Count**

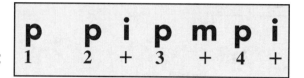

Here is the clawhammer pattern applied to a C chord.

 32

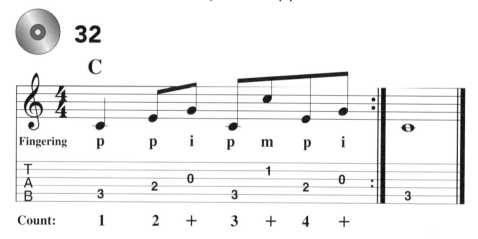

Once you are confident playing this pattern apply it to other chords as in the example below.

 33 In bars 7 and 8 the open third string is used as a bass note and played by **p** on the 2nd and 4th beats.

Fingerpicking Pattern 6

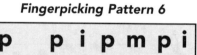

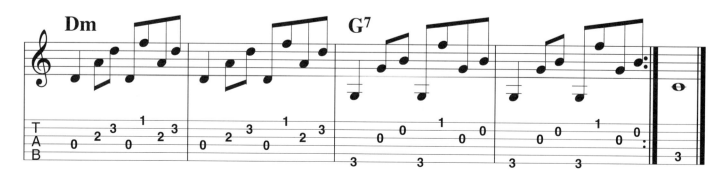

34 Marianne

Use this clawhammer pattern to accompany the melody of
the song Marianne, which is a Caribbean folk song.

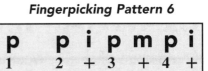

Fingerpicking Pattern 6

LESSON EIGHT

CLAWHAMMER WITH PINCH

A variation of the clawhammer pattern that sounds interesting is to play another note with the middle (m) finger at the same time as the first thumb (p) note ie: $_p^m$. This technique is called the **pinch**.

Fingerpicking Pattern **7a** Count

$_p^m$ indicates that the thumb (**p**) and middle (**m**) fingers play together. Here is pattern 7a applied to a C chord.

35

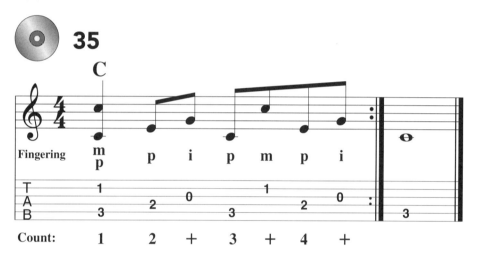

The next chord progression contains chords that are based upon the **C** and **Am** chord shapes.

C 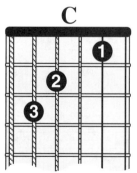 **Cmaj7** **C add9**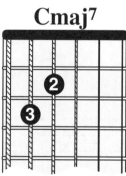

Am  **Am add9**  **Asus**

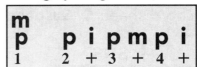

Fingerpicking Pattern 7a

36

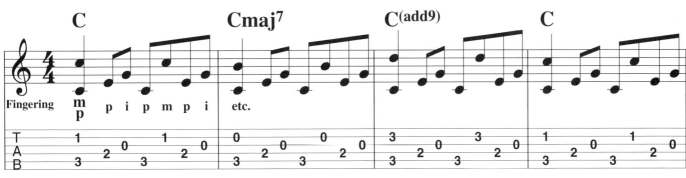

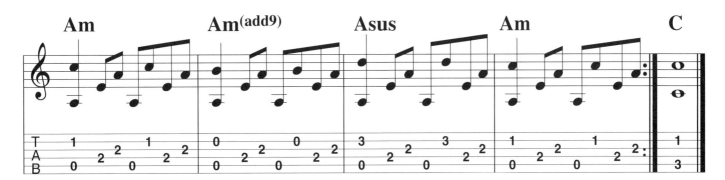

TWO BAR CLAWHAMMER PATTERN

The following clawhammer pattern extends over 2 Bars.

Fingerpicking Pattern 7b

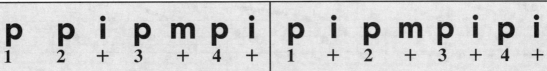

37

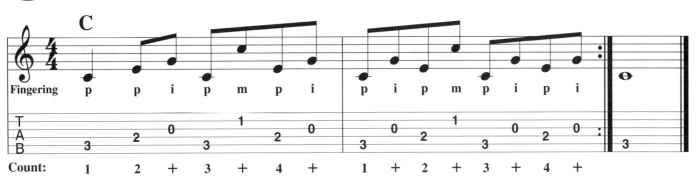

Apply this two bar pattern to the following chord progression which introduces a new chord shape **C Suspended** (C sus).

Csus

The number **2** in the **white circle** indicates that you hold this note even though it is not part of the Csus chord. This will make the chord change from Csus to C easier.

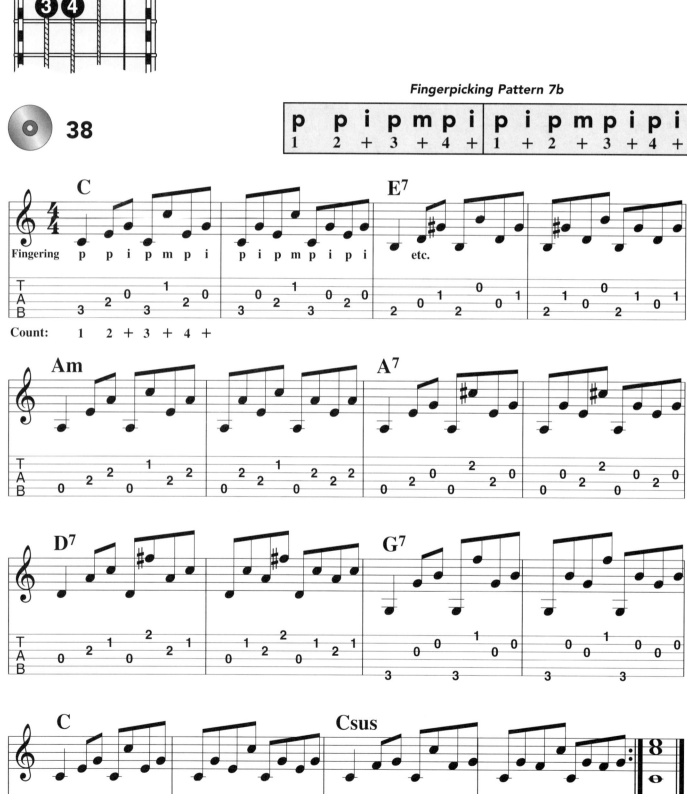

Fingerpicking Pattern 7b

LESSON NINE

THE HAMMER-ON

A **hammer-on** is a technique where the first note is picked but the second note sound is produced by "hammering" the left hand finger onto the fretboard. The hammer-on is indicated on the music staff by a curved line joining two different notes. In Tab notation the hammer-on is indicated by a curved line and the letter **H** above it.

The hammer-on is performed by playing the first note (in the example below - a **C** note on the first fret of the second string) with the **m** finger. While this note is still sounding, the third finger of the left hand hammers down onto the second note (a **D** note on the third fret of the second string). The second note is not picked; the sound is produced entirely by the left hand "hammering" onto the string as shown in the diagrams.

39

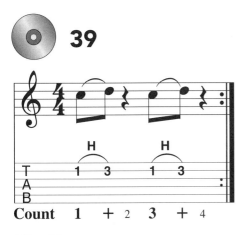

The Hammer-on

Starting position – C note

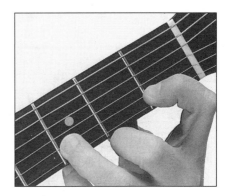

After hammer – D note

THE PULL - OFF

The **pull-off** is like a reverse hammer-on i.e. the first note is picked and the second note sound is created by the finger pulling off the string. In the example below the **D** note is played by the middle (**m**) finger and the **C** note sound is created by the **third** finger pulling off the string. The pull-off is indicated by the letter **P** and a curved line.

40

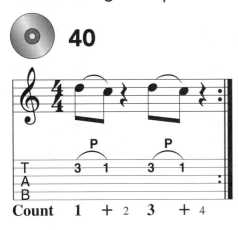

The Pull-off

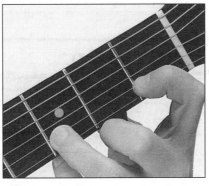

Starting position – D note

After Pull-off – C note

In the examples below the clawhammer pattern is used with hammer-ons and pull-offs. Practice each chord part separately and when confident play the entire progression.

Fingerpicking Pattern 7a

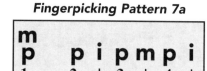

41

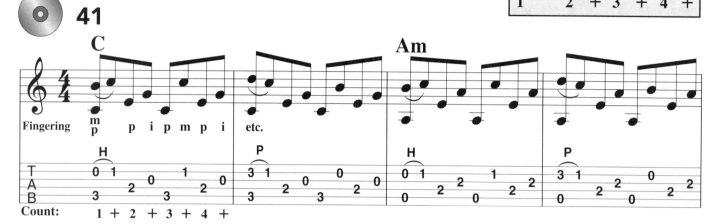

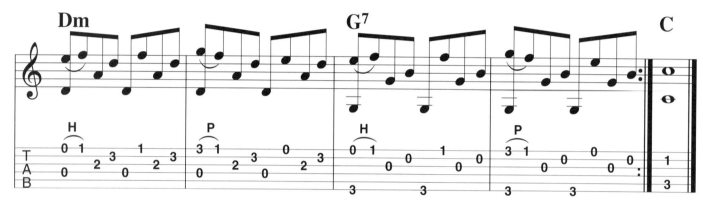

The following progression is based around a **D major** chord.
- **D/C** indicates a **D** chord with a **C** bass note (played by the **second** finger of the left hand).
- **D/B** indicates a **D** chord with a **B** bass note (played by the **first** finger of the left hand).
- The **p** finger also alternates with a bass note on the **3rd** string.

Fingerpicking Pattern 7a

42 This progression is in the **key of D major** as indicated by the key signature which contains two sharps.

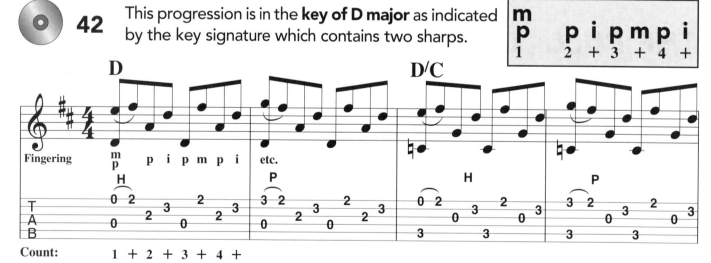

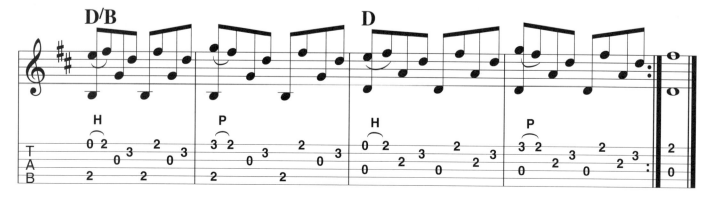

LESSON TEN

SIX STRING CLAWHAMMER

The basic clawhammer pattern uses the **p, m** and **i** fingers. The clawhammer patterns in this lesson also use the **a** finger and can be used to play **all six strings**.

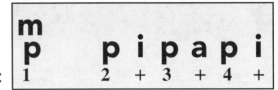

 43

The following example is a turnaround in the key of G and uses fingerpicking pattern 8. Practice this new pattern on each chord separately at first, then play the entire progression. When using the pattern on the C major chord shape, play the **C** and **G** bass notes with the third finger of the left hand alternating between the **5th** and **6th** strings. The other fingers of the left hand remain in position. The D7 chord shape only uses five strings, so you will have to adapt the fingerpicking pattern to fit the chord. Eg: instead of the **a** finger, use **m** as shown below.

This principle will apply to other five string chord shapes such as D, Dm, F, B7 etc.

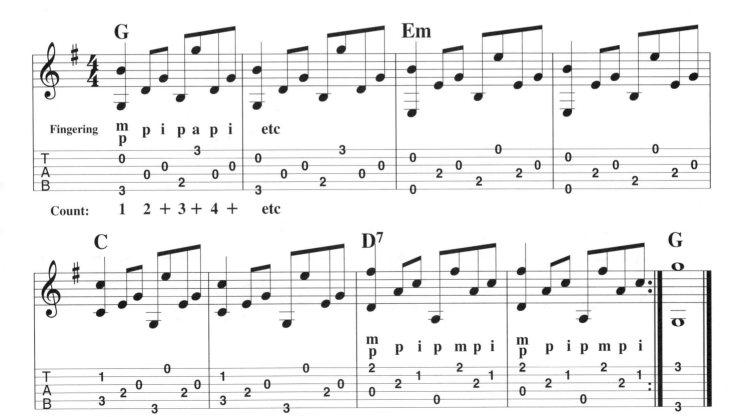

44 El Condor Pasa

This popular South American song is in the **key of E minor**. Use fingerpicking pattern **8** throughout.

Fingerpicking Pattern 8

m		p	i	p	a	p	i
p							
1		2	+	3	+	4	+

45 Camptown Races

Apply the same pattern to the song **Camptown Races**. Pick the bass notes that sound the best to your ear. When playing the **F** chord in bar 11, do not use the **a** finger, but instead use **m** as shown in the pattern 8 variation. Depending on what chord shapes are used to accompany a song, you may have to adapt the fingerpicking patterns to fit.

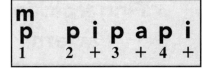

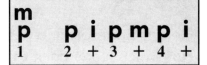

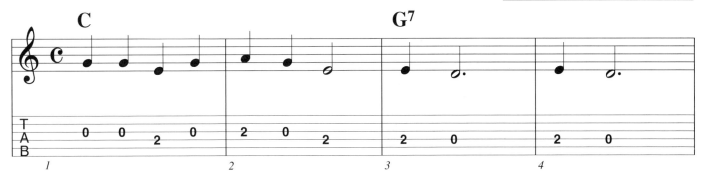

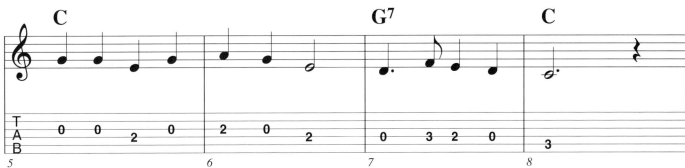

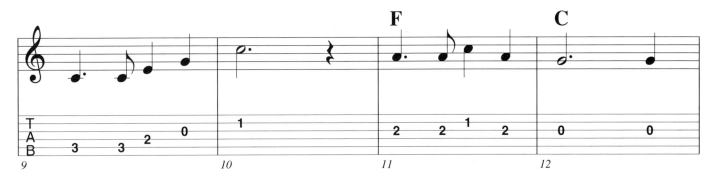

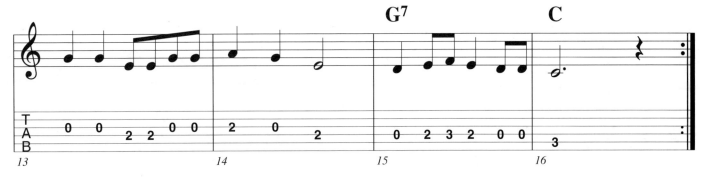

Here is another interesting variation on the clawhammer and pinch technique. Once again all six strings are played.

Fingerpicking Pattern

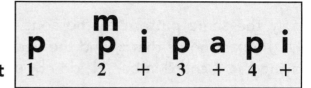

 46

Here is fingerpicking pattern 9 applied to a **C** chord. The second bar contains a **bass note run** which leads back to the same C chord. Bass note runs are played with the thumb (**p**). This bass run is used in the accompaniment to the song **Mussi Den**. Bass note runs can also be used to connect two different chords. Try creating your own bass note runs to connect different chords together.

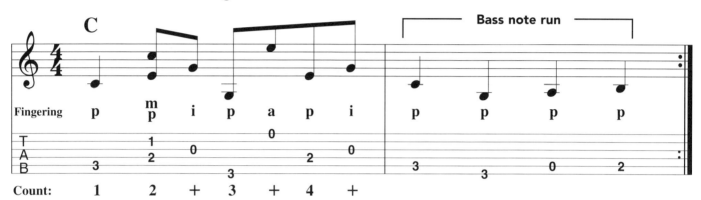

 47 Mussi Den

Fingerpicking Pattern 9

Mussi Den is a well known song from Germany. Try to include some bass note runs in the accompaniment to this song. Listen to the CD for examples of connecting **C** to **Dm** and **G7** to **C**. The **F** and **Dm** chords use only five strings, so adapt the pattern as discussed earlier in the lesson.

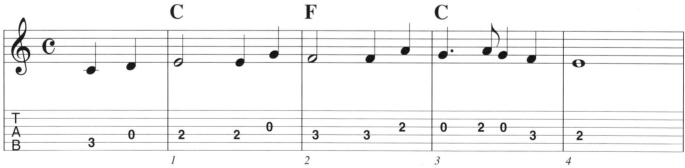

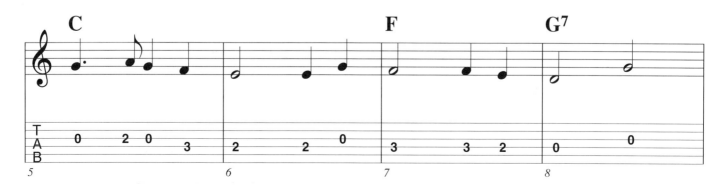

45

LESSON ELEVEN

CLASSICAL GUITAR STYLE

You have now learnt the most important patterns for fingerpicking chord shapes. Fingerstyle guitar can be expanded into accompanying a melody as in the following two classical guitar pieces. If you find this style of playing interesting, see the book **Progressive Classical Guitar Method** for more detail.

48 Spanish Ballad

Fingerpicking Pattern

The fingerpicking pattern for this classical piece is in $\frac{6}{4}$ time and uses only the **p** and **m** fingers.

In $\frac{6}{4}$ time there are **six** quarter notes per bar.

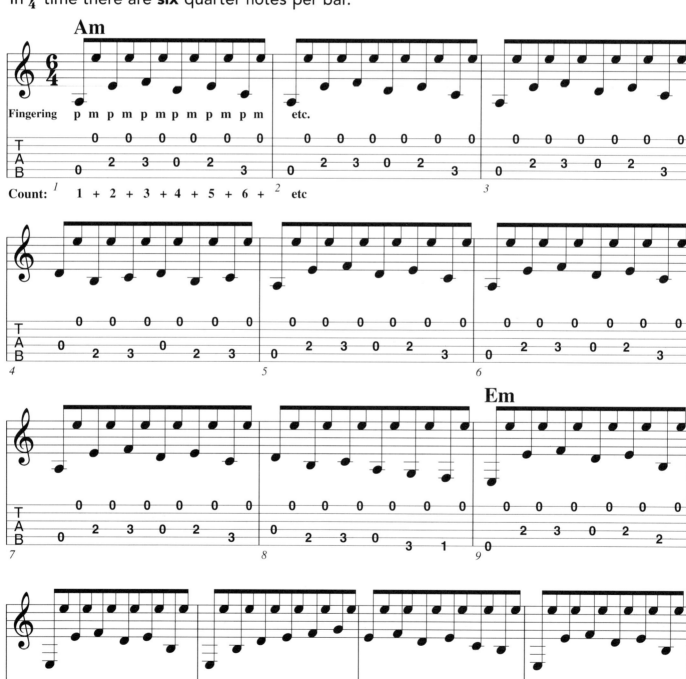

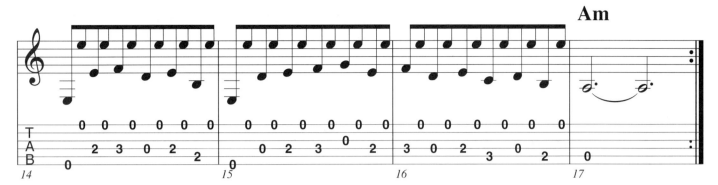

 ## 49 Allegro

This piece uses two different picking patterns which are variations of patterns introduced earlier in this book. Bar 7 introduces a new chord **Am/C**, which is an **Am** chord with a **C bass note**. Left hand finger numbers have been placed next to some of the bass notes to indicate the correct fingering.

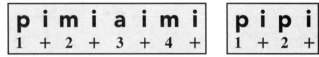

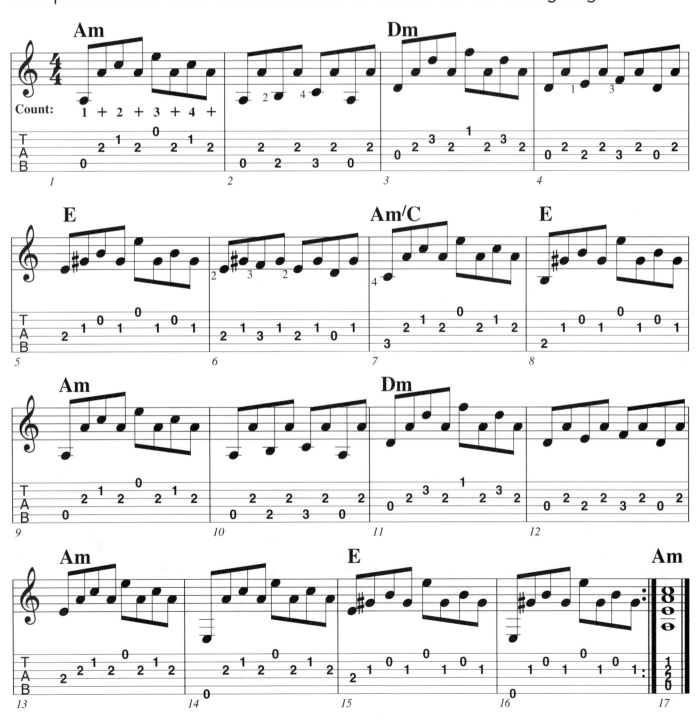

48

The following piece is an arrangement of a popular classical piano piece. See Progressive Popular Classics of the **Great Composers Volumes 1 -6** for more pieces like this.

50 Fur Elise

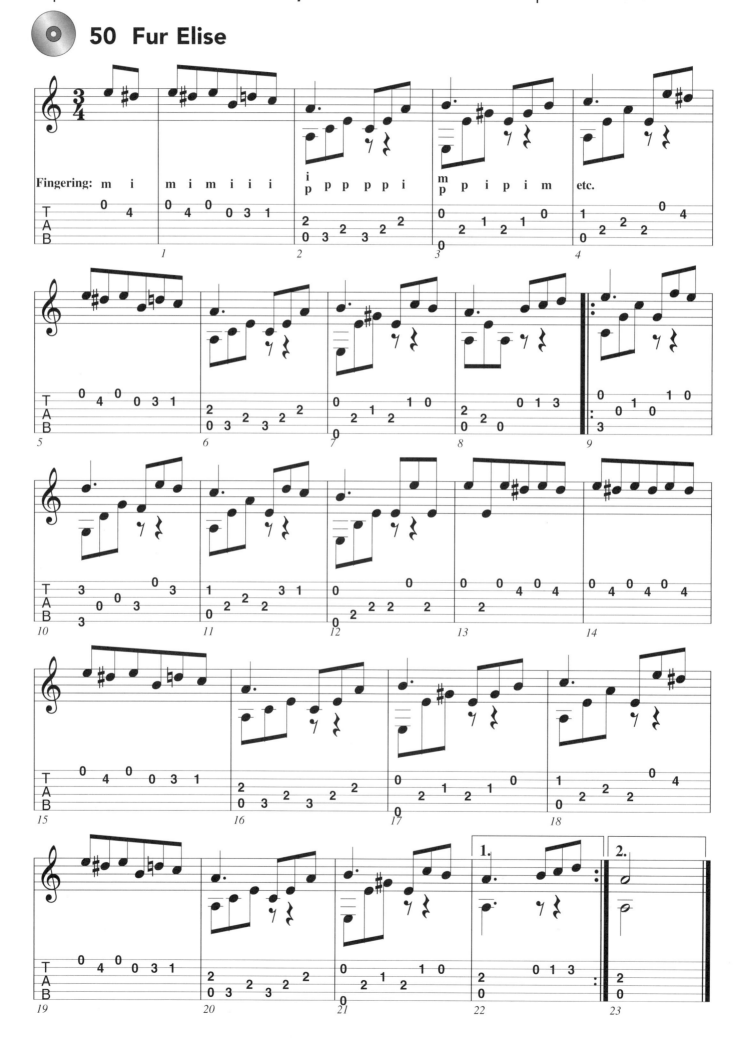

LESSON TWELVE

BLUES FINGERPICKING GUITAR

This lesson introduces another popular fingerpicking style, Blues guitar. The first thing to understand about Blues is common progressions that are often used. The two most frequently used chord progressions in Blues are the 12 Bar and 8 Bar Blues progressions. A Blues progression is generally constructed from the three basic chords in a key which are illustrated in the table below. These three chords are referred to as the **I, IV** and **V** chords. The Roman numerals relating to the **1st, 4th,** and **5th** notes of the major scale from which each chord takes its name. If you find this style of playing interesting, see the book **Progressive Blues Acoustic Guitar Method** for more detail.

Key →	A	A$^\sharp$/B$^\flat$	B	C	C$^\sharp$/D$^\flat$	D	D$^\sharp$/E$^\flat$	E	F	F$^\sharp$/G$^\flat$	G	G$^\sharp$/A$^\flat$
I	A	A$^\sharp$/B$^\flat$	B	C	C$^\sharp$/D$^\flat$	D	D$^\sharp$/E$^\flat$	E	F	F$^\sharp$/G$^\flat$	G	G$^\sharp$/A$^\flat$
IV	D	D$^\sharp$/E$^\flat$	E	F	F$^\sharp$/G$^\flat$	G	G$^\sharp$/A$^\flat$	A	A$^\sharp$/B$^\flat$	B	C	C$^\sharp$/D$^\flat$
V	E	F	F$^\sharp$/G$^\flat$	G	G$^\sharp$/A$^\flat$	A	A$^\sharp$/B$^\flat$	B	C	C$^\sharp$/D$^\flat$	D	D$^\sharp$/E$^\flat$

TWELVE BAR BLUES PROGRESSION

The **twelve bar Blues progression** is the most common chord sequence used in Blues. There are many variations of this progression. The example below consists of four bars of the **I** chord, two bars of the **IV** chord, two bars of the **I** chord, one of the **V** chord, one bar of the **IV** chord and two bars of the **I** chord.

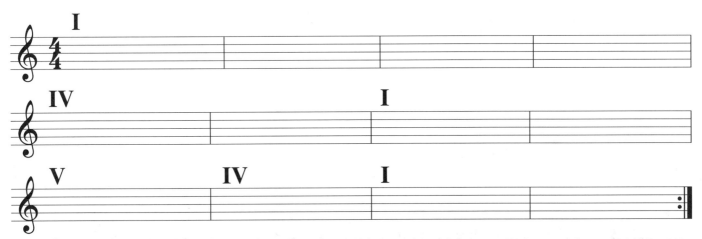

To play the previous progression in the **key of A**, substitute the symbols **I, IV,** and **V** with the three basic chords in the **key of A** (**A, D** and **E**), as shown in the table on the previous page.

To play the first example, use basic chords and use the suggested rhythm pattern. After playing the 12 bars, finish with one strum of the first chord (**A**).

EIGHT BAR BLUES PROGRESSION

CONSTANT BASS LINE

A popular fingerpicking technique that features in Blues guitar is the constant bass line style. This technique involves the right hand thumb playing the root bass note of the chord repeatedly for the duration of the song. The easiest key to apply this style is the key of A because the root bass note of each chord in the key of A (A, D and E) can be played as an open string.

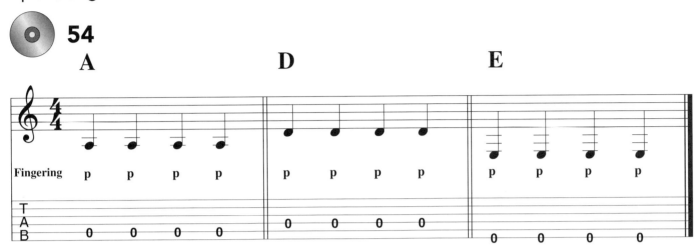

Now try applying the above constant bass lines to a 12 bar Blues progression in the key of A.

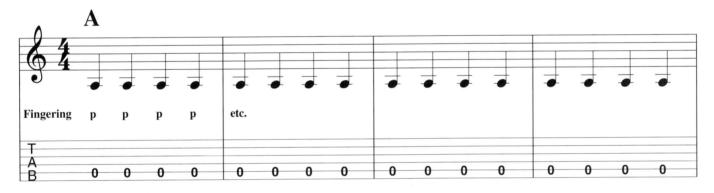

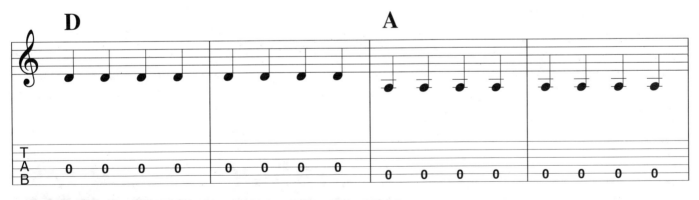

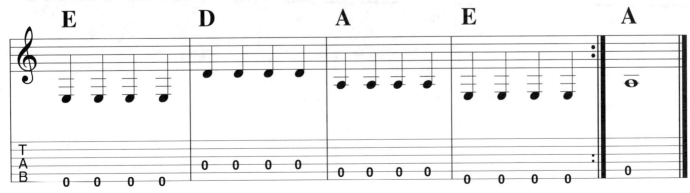

The constant bass line is used in conjuntion with notes from the following A scales.

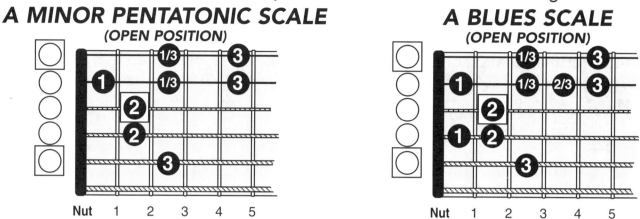

A MINOR PENTATONIC SCALE
(OPEN POSITION)

A BLUES SCALE
(OPEN POSITION)

The next example combines the constant bass line whilst ascending and descending a scale shown above. The recommended fingering should only be used as a guide.

56

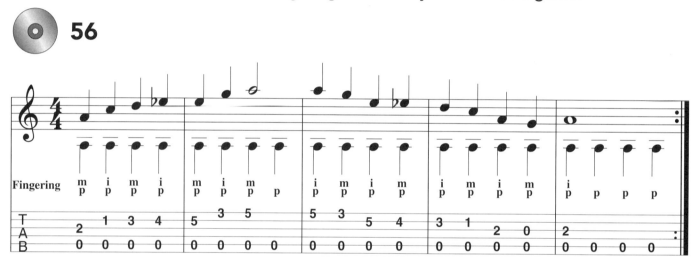

THE SLIDE

This technique involves sliding between two notes on the same string whilst still fretting the string firmly against the fretboard. If played correctly the sound of the second note is produced artificially. The second note is not played with the right hand. The letter "**S**" and a **straight line** indicates a slide. If the line comes from **below** the number, slide from a **lower** fret. If the line comes from **above** the number, slide form a **higher** fret. The number in the brackets is the suggested fret from which to slide from. In this situation the first of the two notes should contain no time value. In the following example a third type of slide is given. A straight line between two tab numbers indicates the first note should be held for a time value before sliding. Listen to the recording to hear the effect of this technique. The accompanying photos illustrate the first and most common type of slides, sliding from a lower fret to a higher fret.

57

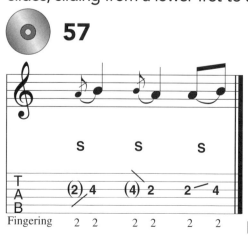

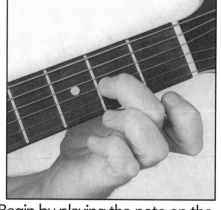

Begin by playing the note on the **second** fret of the **3rd** string.

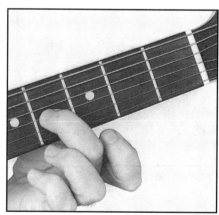

Slide to **fourth** fret, still pressing firmly against fretboard.

The following example is a 12 bar Blues progression in the key of A and uses the constant bass line throughout. It also features use of the slide, hammer-on and pull-off.

58

LESSON THIRTEEN

ALTERNATING THUMB STYLE

The other popular fingerpicking technique used in Blues is the **alternating thumb style**. For this style the thumb alternates between two bass notes on each beat of the bar, usually beginning with the root bass note of the current chord. The three alternating bass lines shown below are for the E, A and B7 chords; i.e. the three principal chords in the key of E.

59

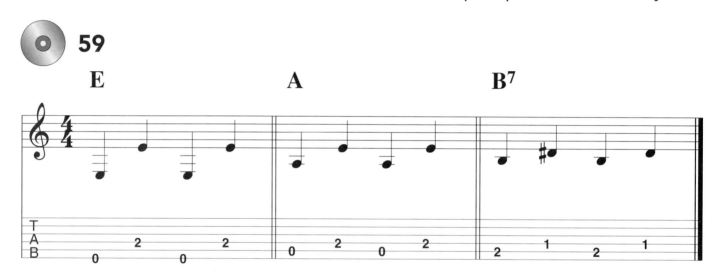

The following exercise combines the alternating thumb stlye with notes based around the E scales that have featured in earlier lessons. When using this style it is common practise to use an alternative fingering for the E major chord. Study accompanying diagram.

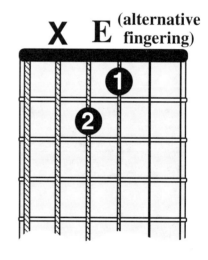

60

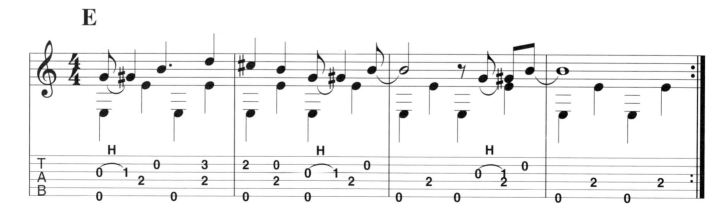

The next two exercises are based upon the A and B7 chords.

A

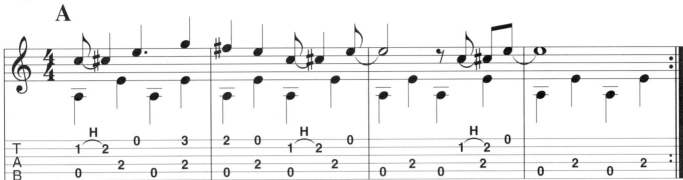

B⁷

The following 8 bar Blues features the alternating thumb style.

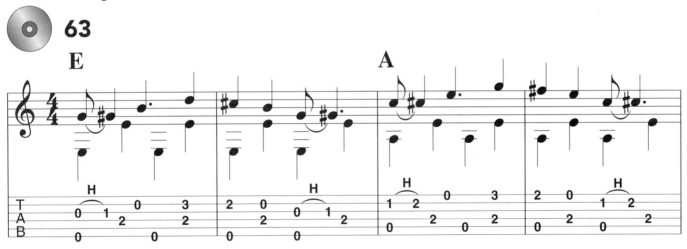

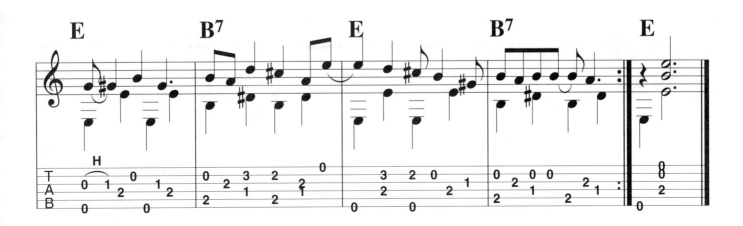

The final example in this lesson is a Blues fingerpicking solo that contains a variety of techniques outlined throughout this book. An alternating thumb style is the basis of this piece but in bars 3, 8 and 9 the bass line changes to a 'walking' bass line. All of the chord shapes that are used are highlighted in the following diagrams. To simplify the music each chord shape is given a number rather than a name.

CHORD SHAPES USED IN EX. 64

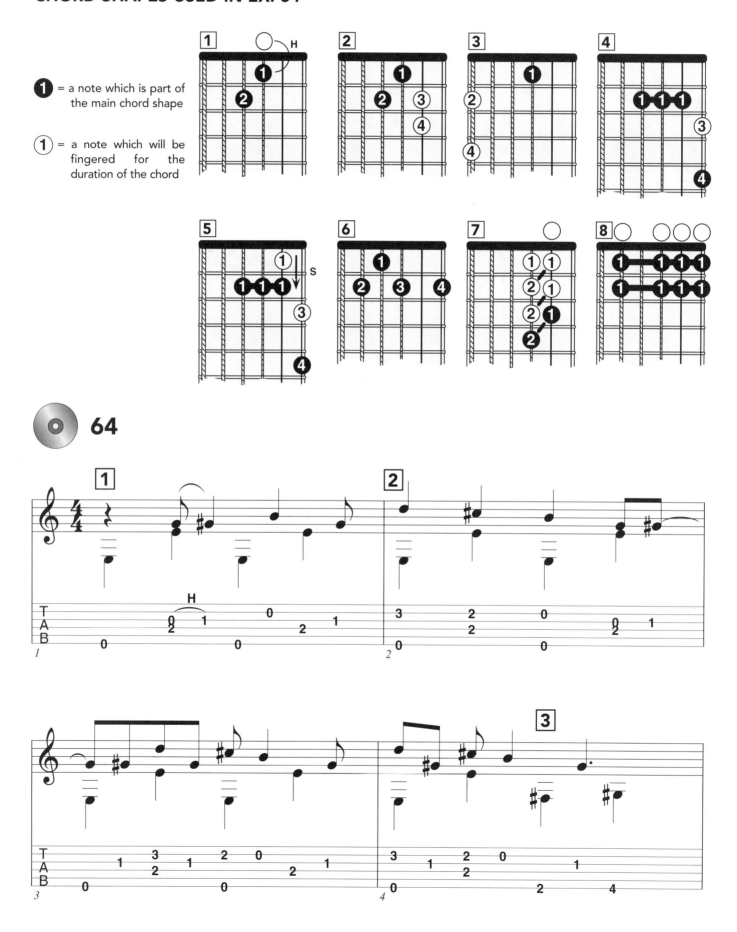

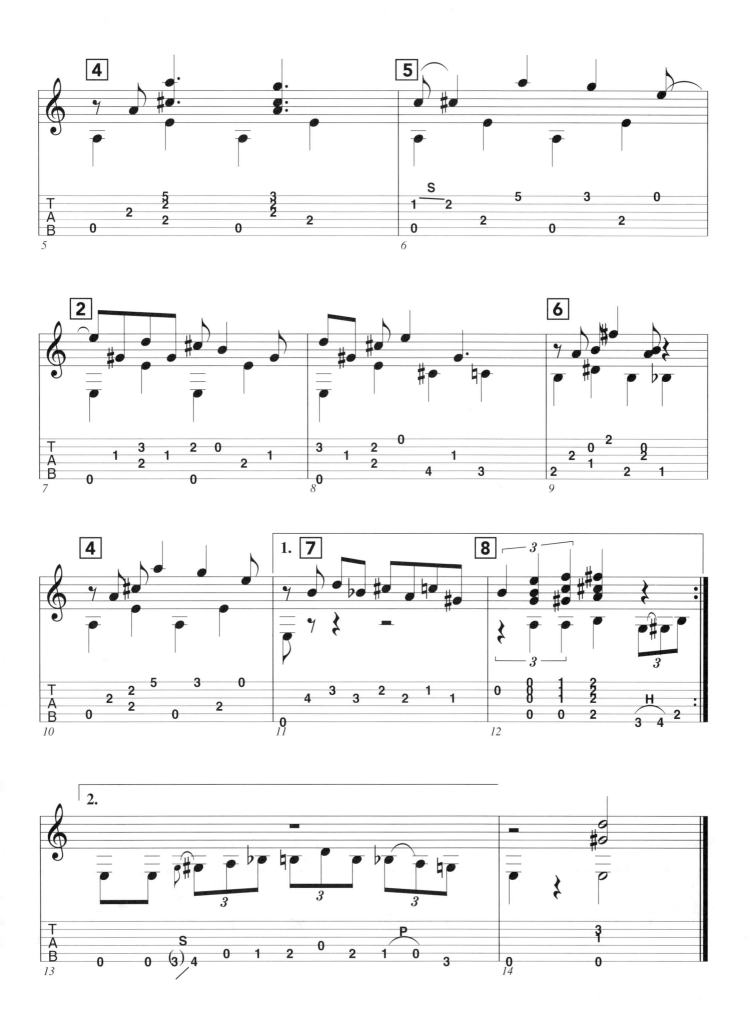

LESSON FOURTEEN

RAGTIME GUITAR

A very popular fingerpicking style is Ragtime. Although Ragtime is mainly played on a piano, the style adapts well to the guitar. The following licks are examples of the Ragtime fingerpicking guitar style.

65

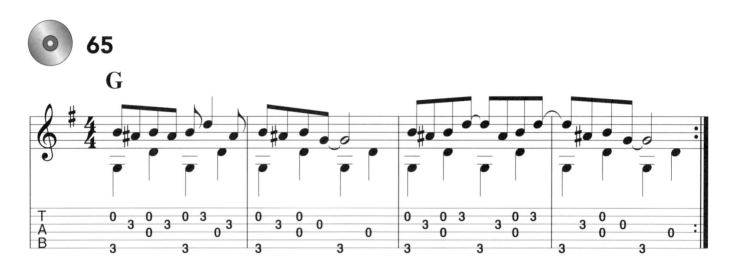

66

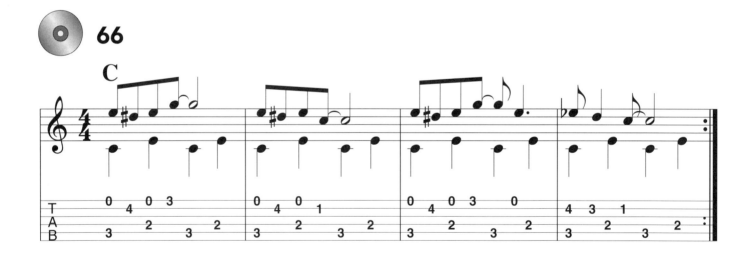

67

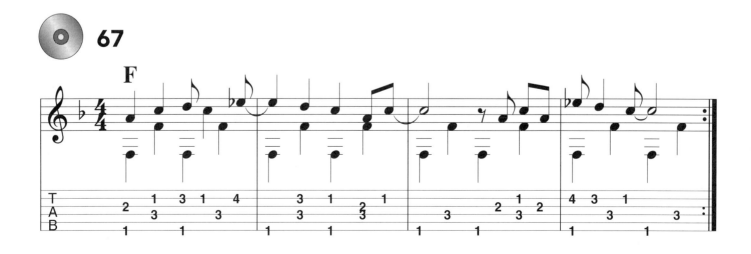

RAGTIME GUITAR SOLO NO. 1 - DETERMINATION RAG

The main chords to the first solo, *Determination Rag* are shown below.

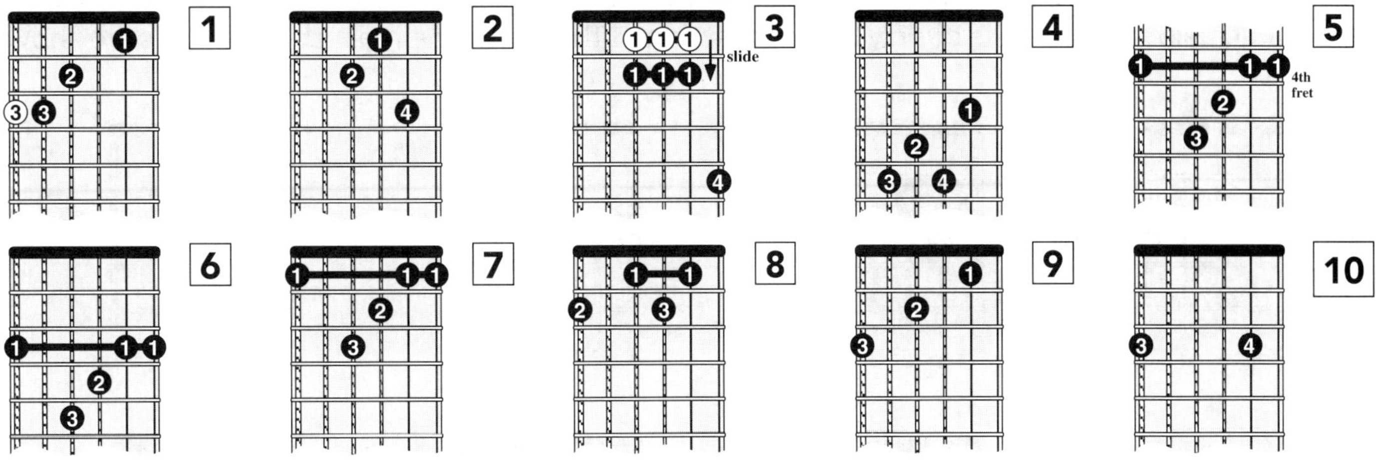

68 Determination Rag

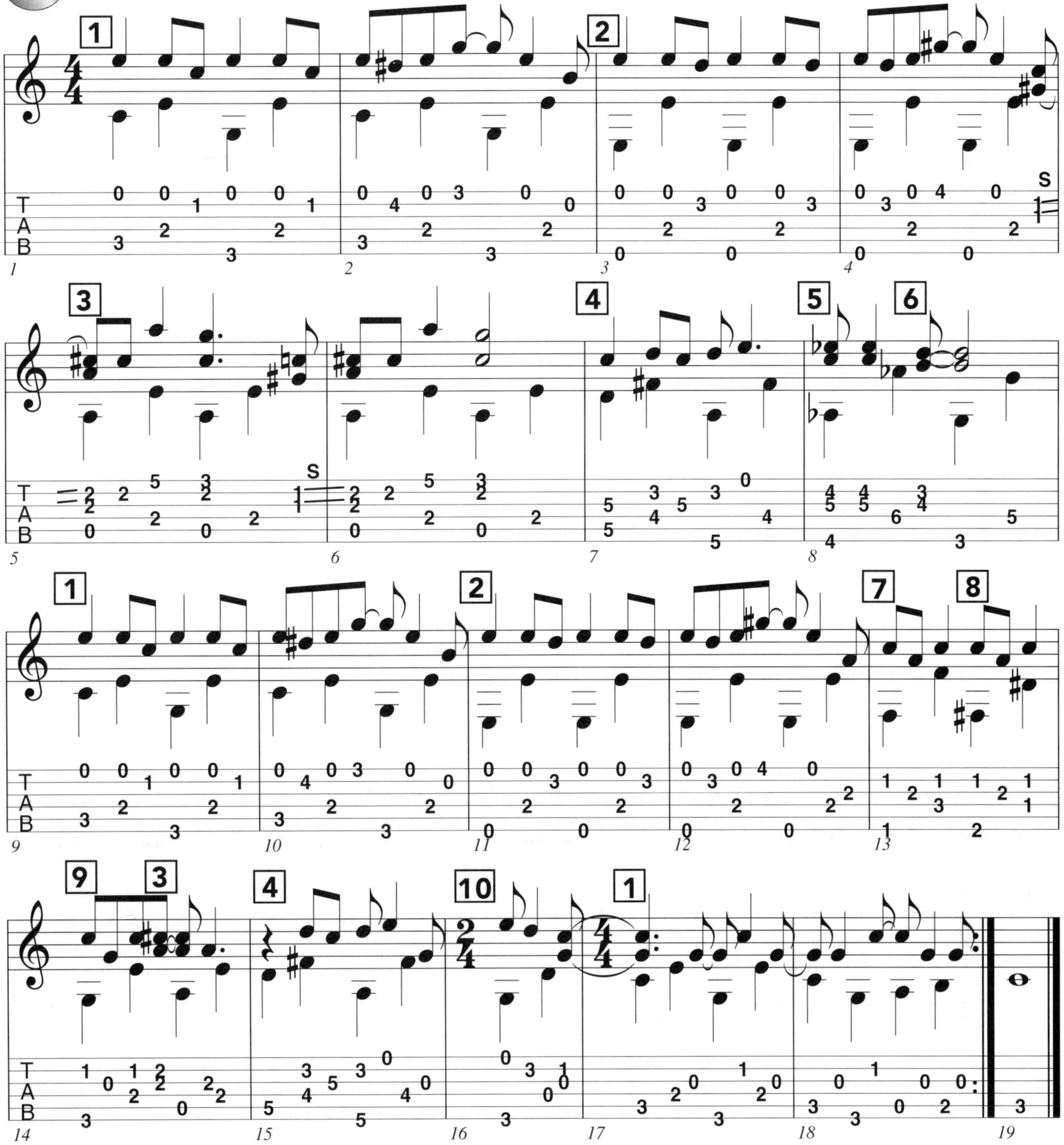

RAGTIME GUITAR SOLO NO. 2 - THE ENTERTAINER

The Entertainer is probably the most well-known of all Ragtime tunes. This arrangement is in the key of G major and consists of only the first section of the song. The main chord shapes are shown below.

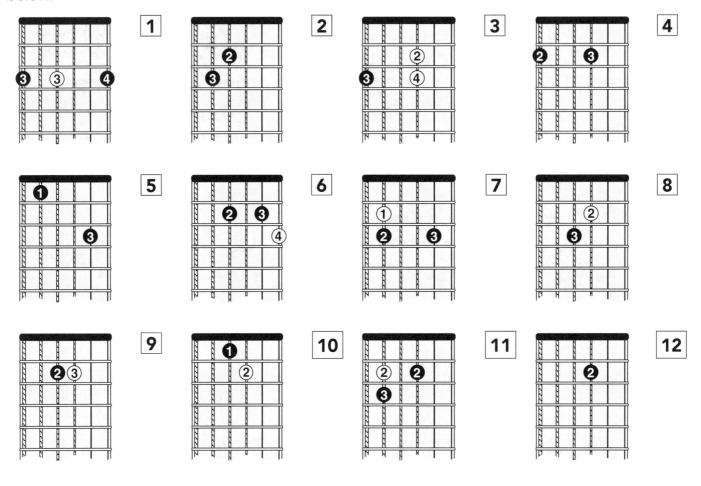

69 The Entertainer

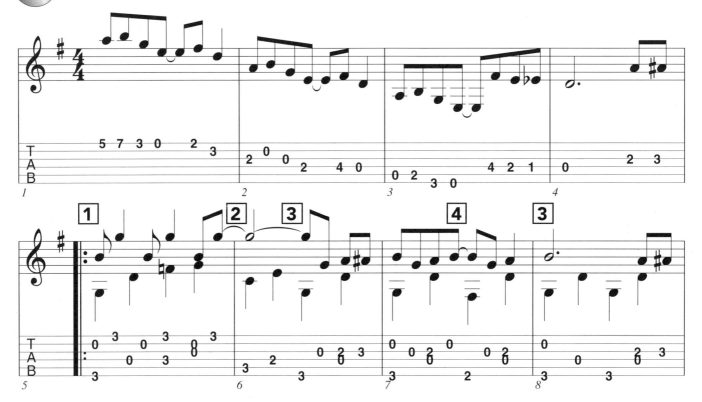

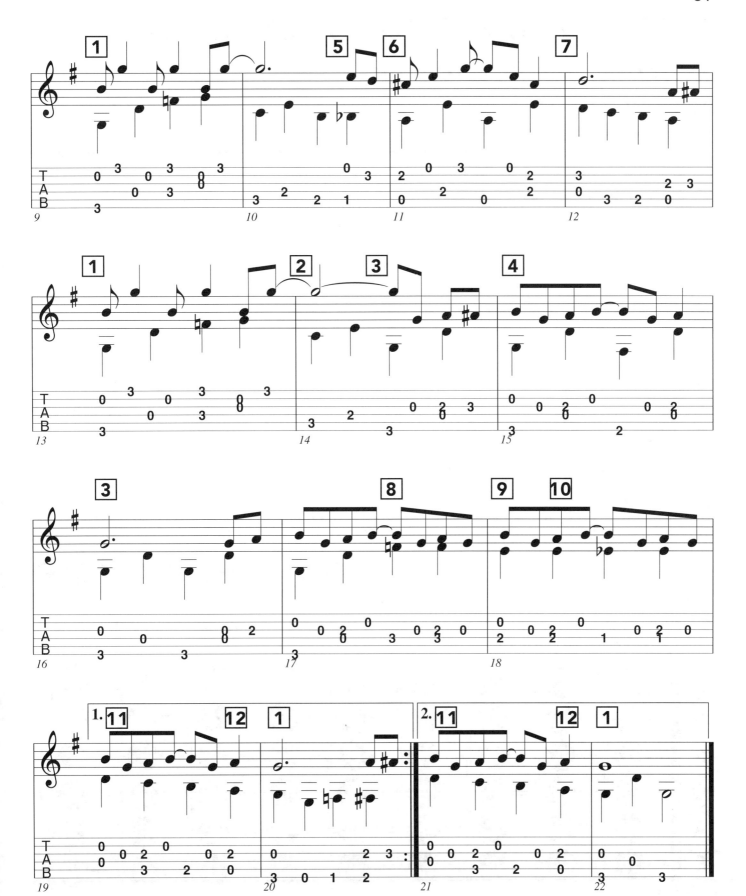

NOTES ON THE GUITAR FRETBOARD

NOTES IN THE OPEN POSITION

The **open position** of the guitar contains the notes of the open strings and the first three frets. Outlined below are the position of these notes on the staff, Tab, and on the fretboard. Also shown is an example of two separate **octaves**, an octave being two notes that have the same letter name and are eight consecutive notes apart. All the songs and examples in this book use notes in the open position.

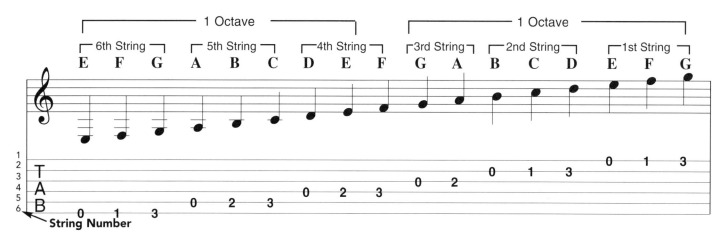

SHARPS AND FLATS

A **sharp** (♯) raises the pitch of a note by one semitone (1 fret). A **flat** (♭) lowers the pitch of a note by one semitone. In music notation the ♯ and ♭ signs are placed before the note on the staff.

Notes on the

Here is a fretboard diagram of all the notes on the guitar. Play the notes on each string the open note e.g. the open 6th string is an **E** note and the note on the 12th fret of the

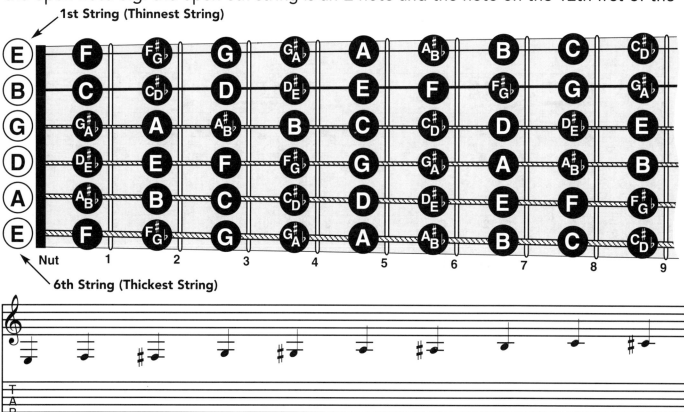

THE CHROMATIC SCALE

With the inclusion of sharps and flats, there are 12 different notes within one octave as shown below.

The notes **EF** and **BC** are always one semitone apart (1 fret). The other notes are a tone apart (2 frets). Sharps (♯) and flats (♭) are found between the notes that are a tone apart:

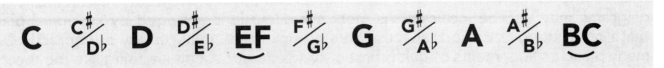

This scale is called the **chromatic scale** and contains all the sharps (♯'s) and flats (♭'s) possible. **C sharp** (**C♯**) has the same position on the fretboard as **D flat** (**D♭**). They are the same note but can have different names depending upon what key you are playing in. The same applies to **D♯** / **E♭**, **F♯** / **G♭**, **G♯** / **A♭** and **A♯** / **B♭**. These are called **enharmonic notes**. Written below are all the notes on the **guitar** including these sharps and flats.

Also notice that:

The **5th fret of the 6th string** (A note) is the same note as the **open 5th string**.
The **5th fret of the 5th string** (D note) is the same note as the **open 4th string**.
The **5th fret of the 4th string** (G note) is the same note as the **open 3rd string**.
The **4th fret of the 3rd string** (B note) is the same note as the **open 2nd string**.
The **5th fret of the 2nd string** (E note) is the same note as the **open 1st string**.

These note positions are important to remember because they are the basis for tuning your guitar to itself (see **Progressive Guitar Method: Book 1**).

All the notes on each of the six strings are shown on the fretboard diagram below. All the notes on the 6th string have been notated on a music staff and TAB below the fretboard diagram.

Guitar Fretboard

from the open notes to the 12th fret. The note on the 12th fret is one octave higher than 6th string is also an **E** note, but is one octave higher.

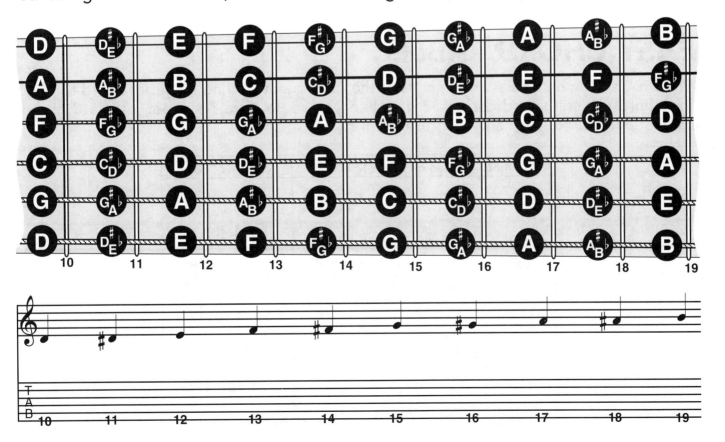

HOW TO READ SHEET MUSIC

Most of the sheet music you will buy will be arranged for piano. Piano music is written using two or three staves, with the chord symbols written above the top staff. It may also contain unfamiliar symbols and terms. At this stage you need only look at the top staff, which contains the melody line (tune), the lyrics and the chords. In some sheet music chord diagrams may also be included. As most sheet music is arranged by keyboard players quite often the guitar chord shapes given are incorrect, unnecessary or impractical, and many piano arrangements of guitar based songs do not sound anything like the recorded version. Guitar tablature versions of sheet music are gradually becoming more popular and in many cases are very accurate arrangements of the song.

Also many piano arrangements are in difficult keys for a beginning guitarist and quite often use unnecessary chords. Piano sheet music also gives no indication of how to strum or fingerpick the chords. So piano sheet music is only a guide for a guitarist but is useful for lyrics and a general chord guide.

If the song contains chords that you are not familiar with you can:

1. **Learn how to play this new chord.**
    Refer to the chord chart on pages 66 and 67 or consult other books in the *Progressive Guitar Method* series e.g. *Progressive Guitar Method: Chords.*
2. **Substitute an easier chord.**
    Use the easy chord table below which lists the type of chord you may see in the sheet music (on the left of the table) and the simpler chord you can substitute (on the right of the table). If you know how to transpose and substitute chords you can play almost every song ever written using only a few basic chord shapes. It is recommended that you do further chord study and at least learn how to play bar chords. Other important chord types to learn are **major seventh (maj7), sixth (6), minor seventh (m7), suspended (sus), diminished (dim) and augmented (+) chords**. All these chords can be found in *Progressive Guitar Method: Chords* and *Progressive Guitar Method: Bar Chords.*

EASY CHORD TABLE

When you see an unfamiliar chord, consult the table below to find an easier chord to play. This chord will still sound correct. E.g., when you see a **Cmaj7** symbol, play a **C** chord instead. For a **Cm6**, you can substitute a **Cm** chord, etc.

Chord Written on Sheet Music			Use This Chord
7	-	Seventh	**Major**
6	-	Sixth	
maj7	-	Major Seventh	
sus	-	Suspended	
9	-	9th	**Seventh (7)**
11	-	Eleventh	
13	-	Thirteenth	
m6	-	Minor Sixth	**Minor (m)**
m7	-	Minor Seventh	
m(maj)7	-	Minor Major Seventh	

3. **Change the key of the song**.
    Transposing (or **Transposition**) is the process of changing a song or piece of music from one key to another.

    There are two reasons for transposing into another key:
    A. If the song is too high or too low to sing, the song can be changed into a lower or higher key. Changing the key of a song does not change the sound, pattern or timing of the melody but simply changes how high or how low it is sung. On page 12 Aura Lee is given in the key of **C major** but on page 29 it is given in the key of **G major** which has lowered the melody. If you sing this transposed melody an octave higher it will still be in the key of G major, but will now be higher to sing than it was in the key of C. So transposing Aura Lee from the key of C to the key of G can make the melody higher or lower to sing.

    B. If the song is hard to play or contains difficult chords you can transpose it to a key with easier chords. e.g. If a song is written in the key of **B♭** (which many songs are) it would contain chords like **B♭**, **E♭** and **Cm** which may be difficult for a beginning guitarist. If the song is transposed into the key of G major the chords would then be **G**, **C** and **Am**, which are easier for a guitarist to play.

HOW TO TRANSPOSE

If the sheet music is in the key of **E flat** (**E♭**) **major** and contains difficult chord shapes, you can transpose it to another major key with easier chord shapes. Keys that contain easy shapes for beginners are **C major** and **G major**, or if the song is in a minor key, **A minor** (**Am**) or **E minor** (**Em**).
Write down the chromatic scale of the key the sheet music is in (usually the first chord is the key chord). Then underneath it write down the chromatic scale of the key you wish to change to. E.g. to change a song from the key of **E♭** to the key of **G**, write down the chromatic scale starting with the note **E♭** and then underneath it write down the chromatic scale starting on the note **G**.

E♭ chromatic scale:	E♭	E	F	G♭	G	A♭	A	B♭	B	C	D♭	D	E♭
G chromatic scale:	G	G#	A	A#	B	C	C#	D	D#	E	F	F#	G

The letter name of the chord is written on the top line and the letter name of the new chord in the new key (in this case **G**) will be directly underneath it.

Note that the chord type never changes. If the chord is a minor chord in the key of **E♭ major** it will also be a minor chord in the major key it is transposed to.

e.g. an **E♭** chord in the key of **E♭ major** becomes a **G** chord in the key of **G major**.
e.g. an **A♭** chord in the key of **E♭ major** becomes a **C** chord in the key of **G major**.
e.g. a **Cm** chord in the key of **E♭ major** becomes an **Em** chord in the key of **G major**.
e.g. a **B♭m** chord in the key of **E♭ major** becomes a **Dm** chord in the key of **G major**.

The easiest keys for fingerpicking guitar are:
G major, C major, D major, A major, E major, A minor and **E minor**. These keys contain chords that have open strings in them and are generally easier shapes to hold.

66

CHORD CHART

Here is a chart of the types of chords you will most commonly find in sheet music. The shapes given are all based around the first few frets. The most useful chord shapes are outlined with a box. The other shapes are given for your reference only but in most cases would be better played holding a bar chord shape. Bar chords, although a little difficult at first are ultimately easier and more convenient to play than most of the non-outlined shapes. All good guitarists play bar chords. For more information on bar chords see **_Progressive Guitar Method: Bar Chords_**. The boxed shapes are generally easier to play and should be memorised. These open chords sound particularly good on acoustic guitars and for fingerpicking.

Major Chords

   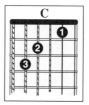 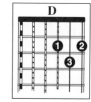
 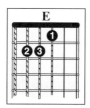 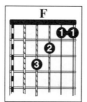 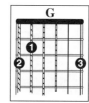

Minor Chords

Chord Symbol **m**

  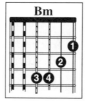   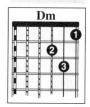
 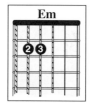

Seventh Chords

Chord Symbol **7**

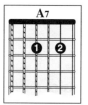 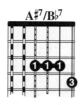 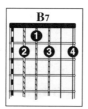 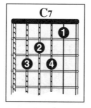 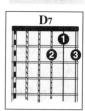
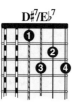 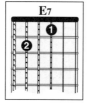   

Minor Seventh Chords

Chord Symbol
m⁷

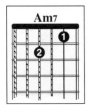 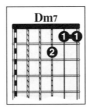 

Major Seventh Chords

Chord Symbol
maj⁷

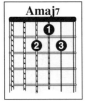  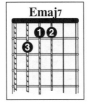  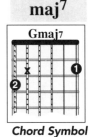

Major Sixth Chords

Chord Symbol
6

 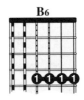 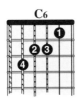  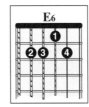 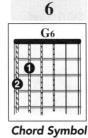

Suspended Chords

Chord Symbol
sus

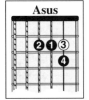 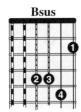  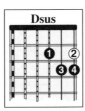  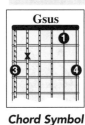

Ninth Chords

Chord Symbol
9

Augmented Chords

Chord Symbol
aug or ⁺

 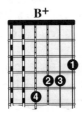 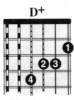   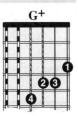

Diminished Chords

Chord Symbol
dim or ⁰

  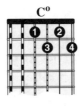    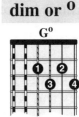

THE CAPO

The **capo** is a device which is placed across the neck of the guitar (acting as a moveable nut). It has 2 uses:

1. To enable the use of easier chord shapes, without changing the key of a song.

2. To change the key of a song, without changing the chord shapes.

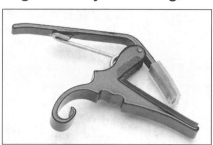

Capos come in various shapes and sizes.

Eg: **1.** If a song is in a key which is within your singing range, but involves playing difficult chord shapes (eg: in the key of **E♭**), a capo may be used. The capo allows you to play the song in the same key, yet at the same time use easier chord shapes. Consider a Turnaround in **E♭**:

If you place the capo on the third fret, the following easier chord shapes can be played without changing the song's key.

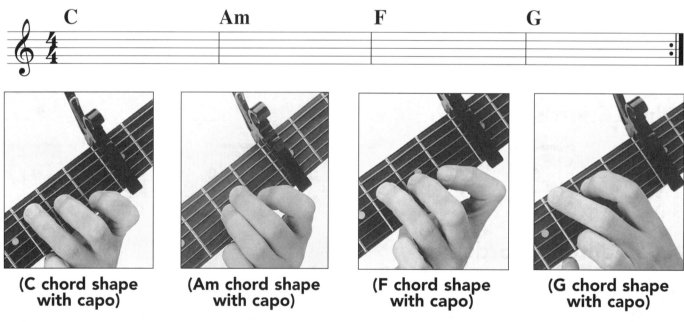

| (C chord shape with capo) | (Am chord shape with capo) | (F chord shape with capo) | (G chord shape with capo) |

If you have studied bar chords, you will notice that the capo is acting as a bar. To work out which fret the capo must be placed on, simply count the number of semitones between the "capo key" you have selected to change to (eg: **C**, as used in the above example) and the original key (i.e. **E♭** as above). Hence **C** to **E♭** = 3 semitones, and therefore the capo must be placed on the third fret.

Eg: **2.** If the song is in a key that already has easy chord shapes but is out of range to sing, you can change the key by placing the capo on a particular fret and still use the easy chord shapes. Eg: if you start with the above Turnaround in the **key of C** but wish to change it to the **key of E♭**, place the capo at the third fret and play the same **C Am F G** chord shapes. When you play these chord shapes with the capo at the third fret they become **E♭ Cm A♭ B♭**.

GLOSSARY OF MUSICAL TERMS

Accidental — a sign used to show a temporary change in pitch of a note (i.e. sharp ♯, flat ♭, double sharp 𝄪, double flat ♭♭, or natural ♮). The sharps or flats in a key signature are not regarded as accidentals.

Ad lib — to be played at the performer's own discretion.

Allegretto — moderately fast.

Allegro — fast and lively.

Andante — an easy walking pace.

Arpeggio — the playing of a chord in single note fashion.

Bar — a division of music occurring between two bar lines (also called a 'measure').

Bar chord — a chord played with one finger lying across all six strings on the guitar.

Bar line — a vertical line drawn across the staff dividing the music into equal sections called bars.

Bass — the lower regions of pitch in general. On guitar, the 4th, 5th and 6th strings.

Chord — a combination of three or more different notes played together.

Chord progression — a series of chords played as a musical unit (e.g. as in a song).

Clef — a sign placed at the beginning of each staff of music which fixes the location of a particular note on the staff, and hence the location of all other notes.

Coda — an ending section of music, signified by the sign ⊕ .

Common time — and indication of $\frac{4}{4}$ time — four quarter note beats per bar (also indicated by 𝄴).

D.C al fine — a repeat from the sign (indicated thus 𝄋) to the word 'fine'.

Dynamics — the varying degrees of softness (indicated by the term 'piano') and loudness (indicated by the term 'forte') in music.

Eighth note — a note with the value of half a beat in $\frac{4}{4}$ time, indicated thus ♪ (also called a quaver).

The eighth note rest — indicating half a beat of silence is written: ♮

Enharmonic — describes the difference in notation, but not in pitch, of two notes.

Fermata — a sign, ⌒ , used to indicate that a note or chord is held to the player's own discretion (also called a 'pause sign').

Flat — a sign, (♭)used to lower the pitch of a note by one semitone.

Forte — loud. Indicated by the sign 𝆑 .

Half note — a note with the value of two beats in $\frac{4}{4}$ time, indicated thus: 𝅗𝅥 (also called a minim). The half note rest, indicating two beats of silence, is written: ▬ on the third staff line.

Harmony — the simultaneous sounding of two or more different notes.

Interval — the distance between any two notes of different pitches.

Key — describes the notes used in a composition in regards to the major or minor scale from which they are taken; e.g. a piece 'in the key of C major' describes the melody, chords, etc., as predominantly consisting of the notes, C, D, E, F, G, A, and B — i.e. from the C scale.

Key signature — a sign, placed at the beginning of each stave of music, directly after the clef, to indicate the key of a piece. The sign consists of a certain number of sharps or flats, which represent the sharps or flats found in the scale of the piece's key.

Leger lines — small horizontal lines upon which notes are written when their pitch is either above or below the range of the staff.

Legato — smoothly, well connected.

Lick — a short musical phrase.

Major scale — a series of eight notes in alphabetical order based on the interval sequence tone - tone - semitone - tone - tone - tone - semitone, giving the familiar sound **do re mi fa so la ti do**.

Melody — a group of notes of varying pitch and duration, and having a recognizable musical shape.

Metronome — a device which indicates the number of beats per minute, and which can be adjusted in accordance to the desired tempo.

Moderato — at a moderate pace.**Natural** — a sign (♮)used to cancel out the effect of a sharp or flat. The word is also used to describe the notes **A, B, C, D, E, F** and **G**; e.g. 'the natural notes'.

Note — a single sound with a given pitch and duration.

Octave — the distance between any given note with a set frequency, and another note with exactly double that frequency. Both notes will have the same letter name.

Open voicing — a chord that has the notes spread out between both hands on the keyboard.

Pitch — the sound produced by a note, determined by the frequency of the string vibrations. The pitch relates to a note being referred to as 'high' or 'low'.

Plectrum — a small object (often of a triangular shape)made of plastic which is used to pick or strum the strings of a guitar.

Position — a term used to describe the location of the left hand on the guitar fret board. The left hand position is determined by the fret location of the first finger. The 1st position refers to the 1st to 4th frets. The 3rd position refers to the 3rd to 6th frets and so on.

Quarter note — a note with the value of one beat in $\frac{4}{4}$ time, indicated thus ♩ (also called a crotchet). The quarter note rest, indicating one beat of silence, is written: 𝄽 .

Repeat signs — used to indicate a repeat of a section of music, by means of two dots placed before a double bar line.

Rhythm — the note after which a chord or scale is named (also called 'key note').

Riff — a repeating pattern which may be altered to fit chord changes.

Semitone — the smallest interval used in conventional music. On guitar, it is a distance of one fret.

Sharp — a sign (♯) used to raise the pitch of a note by one semitone.

Staccato — to play short and detached. Indicated by a dot placed above the note.

Staff — five parallel lines together with four spaces, upon which music is written.

Syncopation — the placing of an accent on a normally unaccented beat.

Tempo — the speed of a piece.

Tie — a curved line joining two or more notes of the same pitch, where the second note(s) is not played, but its time value is added to that of the first note.

Timbre — a quality which distinguishes a note produced on one instrument from the same note produced on any other instrument (also called 'tone colour'). A given note on the guitar will sound different (and therefore distinguishable) from the same pitched note on piano, violin, flute etc. There is usually also a difference in timbre from one guitar to another.

Time signature — a sign at the beginning of a piece which indicates, by means of figures, the number of beats per bar (top figure), and the type of note receiving one beat (bottom figure).

Tone — a distance of two frets; i.e. the equivalent of two semitones.

Transposition — the process of changing music from one key to another.

Treble — the upper regions of pitch in general.

Treble clef — a sign placed at the beginning of the staff to fix the pitch of the notes placed on it. The treble clef (also called 'G clef') is placed so that the second line indicates as G note.

PROGRESSIVE ROCK GUITAR TECHNIQUE
FOR INTERMEDIATE ROCK GUITARISTS

This book continues on from *Progressive Rock Guitar Method*, dealing with all the Rhythm and Lead guitar styles of Rock. Rhythm guitar will be developed further by learning Bar chords, Rock progressions and advanced rhythm techniques. Lead guitarists will learn scale patterns, licks and solos using techniques such as Hammer-ons, Pull-offs, Slides, Bends, Vibrato and Double Note Licks. All licks and solos are clearly notated using standard music notation and 'Easy Read' guitar tab.

PROGRESSIVE BLUES LEAD GUITAR METHOD
FOR BEGINNER TO ADVANCED

This book takes a unique approach to learning Blues lead guitar. The most common scale used in Blues – the minor pentatonic scale, is used immediately to make music. The scale is learned in five basic positions which cover the whole fretboard, along with a variety of licks and solos demonstrating all the important techniques such as slides, vibrato and note bending, as used by all the great Blues players.

PROGRESSIVE LEAD GUITAR LICKS
FOR BEGINNER TO ADVANCED

Features over 110 licks incorporating the styles and techniques used by the world's best lead guitarists. Covers Rock, Blues, Metal, Country, Jazz, Funk, Soul, Rockabilly, Slide and Fingerpicking. Several solos are included to fully show how the licks and techniques can be used to create a lead guitar solo. The emphasis in this volume is to provide a vast variety of music styles to enable you to fit in with any music or recording situation. All licks are clearly notated using standard music notation and 'Easy Read' guitar tab.

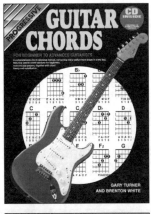

PROGRESSIVE GUITAR CHORDS
FOR BEGINNER TO ADVANCED GUITARISTS

Shows you every useful chord shape in every key. An open chord section for beginners contains the simplest and most widely used chord shapes in all keys. A bar chord section for the semi-advanced player who will need a thorough knowledge of bar chord shapes in all positions. A section for the advanced player listing the moveable shapes for chords widely used by Jazz guitarists. Other sections contain important music theory for the guitarist including scales, keys and chord construction.

PROGRESSIVE BLUES RHYTHM GUITAR TECHNIQUE
FOR INTERMEDIATE BLUES GUITARISTS

Features great rhythm parts in a wide variety of Blues and R&B styles including shuffles, boogie, jump Blues, traditional slow Blues, Rock and Roll, Jazz and Funk. Shows you how to create rhythm parts using both chords and single note riffs and how to fit your parts to the style and instrumental combination you are playing with. Anyone who completes this book will be well on the way to being a great rhythm player.

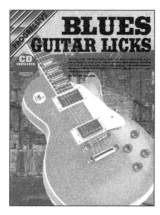

PROGRESSIVE BLUES GUITAR LICKS
FOR BEGINNER TO ADVANCED
Packed full of Blues guitar licks and solos incorporating styles and techniques used by the world's greatest Blues players. Includes sections on turnarounds, intro's and endings, call and response, dynamics and learning from other instruments. The licks cover a variety of styles such as shuffles, traditional slow Blues, Boogie, Jazz style Blues and R&B and Funk grooves. Also includes examples demonstrating how different licks can be put together to form whole solos, opening up endless possibilities for improvisation.

PROGRESSIVE BLUES GUITAR SOLOS
INTERMEDIATE TO ADVANCED
Contains a great selection of Blues solos in a variety of styles reflecting the whole history of the Blues tradition from early Delta Blues to contemporary Blues Rock. Demonstrates various methods of creating solos along with sections on vocal style phrasing, call and response, developing a theme, dynamics and the use of space. Many of the solos are written in the styles of Blues legends like Muddy Waters, John Lee Hooker, BB, Albert and Freddy King, Buddy Guy, Albert Collins, Peter Green, Magic Sam, Otis Rush, Eric Clapton and Stevie Ray Vaughan.

PROGRESSIVE ROCK GUITAR LICKS
FOR INTERMEDIATE TO ADVANCED
This book may be used by itself or as a useful supplement to *Progressive Rock Guitar Technique*. The licks throughout the book are examples of how the most popular lead guitar patterns can be used in all positions on the fretboard, and how various techniques can be applied to each pattern. Several Rock guitar solos are included to fully show how the licks and techniques studied throughout the book can be used to create a solo.

PROGRESSIVE SCALES AND MODES FOR GUITAR
FOR BEGINNER TO ADVANCED
Progressive Scales and Modes gives the student a complete system for learning any scale, mode or chord and makes it easy to memorize any new new sound as well as building a solid visual and aural foundation of both the theory and the guitar fretboard. The book also shows you how to use each scale as well as how and why it fits with a particular chord or progression. The final section contains jam along progressions for every scale and mode presented in the book.

PROGRESSIVE FUNK AND R&B GUITAR TECHNIQUE
INTERMEDIATE TO ADVANCED
Covers a range of exciting chord sounds essential to Funk, along with the Dorian and Mixolydian modes and the use of harmonic intervals such as 6ths, 3rds, 4ths, octaves and tritones. Also features a thorough study of rhythms and right hand techniques such as percussive strumming and string muting. A range of Funk styles are examined, as well as some great Soul and R&B sounds.